CORVETTE

CORVETTE
PORTRAIT OF A LEGEND

RICHARD LANGWORTH
with contributions from
Kevin Brazendale, Jerry Burton and Graham Jones

GALLERY BOOKS
An Imprint of W. H. Smith Publishers Inc.
112 Madison Avenue
New York City 10016

© Macdonald & Co (Publishers) Ltd 1989

First published in Great Britain in 1989
by Macdonald & Co (Publishers) Ltd
London & Sydney

A member of Maxwell Pergamon Publishing Corporation plc

First published in the United States in 1989
by Gallery Books, an imprint of W.H. Smith Publishers, Inc.,
112 Madison Avenue, New York 10016

Gallery Books are available for bulk purchase for sales
promotions and premium use. For details write or telephone
the Manager of Special Sales, W.H. Smith Publishers, Inc.,
112 Madison Avenue, New York, New York 10016. (212) 532-6600

Typeset by Flairplan Phototypesetting Ltd, Ware, Hertfordshire
Printed in Italy by OFSA SpA, Milan
Bound in Italy by Legatoria Editoriale Giovanni Olivotto

Text commissioned and edited by CW Editorial Limited
538 Ipswich Road, Slough, Berkshire SL1 4EQ

Designed by Alan Gooch
Mander Gooch Callow, 7 Hanover Street, London W1R 9HH

'Fiberglass Fantasy: The Marketing of the Chevrolet Corvette' written by
Jerry Burton, Editor of *Corvette Quarterly*
'Pioneers of Perfection: A Technical History' written by
Kevin Brazendale, Deputy Editor of *Performance Tuning*
'In a Class of Its Own: Corvette Comparisons' written by
Graham Jones, Motorsports Editor of the *Toronto Star*

Project editor: Gillian Prince
Senior production controller: Sonya Sibbons
Art director: Linda Cole

ISBN 0-8317-1787-4

Dedicated to the memory of

Sam Folz

Enthusiast, Teacher, Friend

CONTENTS

CONTENTS

PAGE 9 The distinctive Chevrolet Corvette badge, recognized by *aficionados* everywhere.

PREVIOUS SPREAD The first generation Corvette lasted from 1953 to 1955 (this is a '55 model) and set the Corvette trend of a fiberglass-bodied rear-drive sports car that is still followed to this day.

FACING PAGE & ABOVE Chevrolet were one step up on their British sports car rivals in offering fully trimmed interiors. The 265cu in V8 appeared in 1955, giving 225bhp, replacing the original 'Blue Flame' straight-six.

FOLLOWING SPREAD The '55 model was virtually unchanged visually from the '54 as various proposed facelifts were not adopted by Chevrolet management.

FACING PAGE 17 The 1954 Motorama show cars were proposed production Corvettes, but poor sales of the existing cars meant they came to naught, although the Nomad station wagon design entered production in the Chevrolet Bel Air range, and as the similar Pontiac Safari of 1955–57.

ORIGIN
OF THE
SPECIES

1953 – 1955

THE Corvette may be the all-American sports car but, curiously, Great Britain had a lot to do with the origins of the Corvette; so, if you carry the thought far enough, did Adolf Hitler. Had it not been for Der Führer, there would have been no World War II; had there not been a war there would not have been several million GIs stationed in or passing through Britain afterwards. Back home, those former servicemen spawned America's interest in and demand for sporting two-seaters, which in turn convinced General Motors that a post-war sports car might actually sell well enough to justify its production.

Some locals complained that the Yanks were 'oversexed, overpaid, overfed and over here', but the GIs generally loved Britain. And one of the things they liked best, after the war, was the English sports car. There are no statistics on it, but odds favor the thesis that the most popular souvenirs of England for returning American servicemen were MG TCs, Jaguar XK120s, or any of the score of lesser-known sports cars offered by a reviving British motor industry. Here was the genesis of that popular movement in American

motoring circles which culminated in the Chevrolet Corvette.

Contrary to popular belief, American automotive history is replete with sports cars, although near-barren of them between 1930 and 1950. Sparse-bodied two-seaters, hung on chassis as primitive as the Model T Ford's and as sophisticated as the Packard's, had been built in the States almost from the beginning of the horseless carriage; Americans raced them, at venues ranging from primitive dirt tracks to purpose-built wood-planked raceways, to the huge brick-paved oval of Indianapolis — a race course built just three years after the world's first at Brooklands. By 1910, serious manufacturers like Peerless, Chadwick, Simplex and Pierce had 'production' sports cars any wealthy young blade could buy ready-to-run. Imagine if you can the Pierce 66 two-passenger runabout, on a massive 147.5-inch wheelbase, priced at the equivalent in today's money of $250,000.

The two greatest American sports cars of that age were the Mercer Raceabout and the Stutz Bearcat: Roarers from the Roaring Twenties knew them well. The last Raceabouts were built in 1915, but a decade later they were still serving as dual-purpose race-and-ride sports cars, capable of running all day at 75mph, an astonishing speed for the time. Modern writers have commented fulsomely on the Raceabout's remarkably civilized character despite its age, one being reminded 'of a rather large Morgan'. The last Stutz Bearcat, with its sixteen-valve, 88bhp, 6-litre, *four-cylinder* engine, could hit 90mph.

The Great Depression of the 1930s put paid to the sports-car urges of Americans. Not that everyone was broke — they weren't. But it was not considered good form to indulge in such aristocratic pleasures as sports-car racing, or to be seen in too rakish a motor car. The few premium-priced cars still built tended to be conservative closed models; thanks to replica bodies, there are far more open Duesenbergs in existence today than Duesenberg's original customers ever commissioned.

The Depression was felt just as hard in Britain, but the island race took a different view of matters automotive. The UK industry continued to build fast, light two-seaters, which competed in such varied events as 'trials' and the Monte Carlo Rally. The 1939–45 war had no sooner ended than British companies which had survived in good shape got back into production with those same cars. The Labour Government encouraged heavy emphasis on exports — and the visiting Americans were the best customers. As they returned from England in the late '40s, many of them packed an MG, Allard, Healey Silverstone, Riley, Lea Francis or — after 1948 — a Jaguar XK120, which became a legend in its own time.

Back home, these enthusiasts found the kernel of a sports-car movement intact. The Automobile Racing Club of America had been founded before the war by the famous racing Collier brothers, Sam and Miles, and transformed in 1944 to the Sports Car Club of America. Interestingly, ARCA's original emblem had been designed for the Colliers by a young GM stylist the Corvette world

would hear much of later: Bill Mitchell.

Through 1949, the US motor industry was too occupied meeting pent-up demand for ten million new family cars to worry much about sports models. However, by the 1950s, flush with postwar profits and urged on by a small but vociferous sports-car fraternity, the moguls began to lay plans. Nash and Donald Healey teamed to produce the impressive, Le Mans-competitive Nash-Healey in 1951; Kaiser decided in 1952 to build the fiberglass Darrin with its sliding doors; Ford, by 1953, were studying Nash-Healeys, Jaguars and MGs with an eye to building what eventually would become the Thunderbird; privateers like Earl 'Madman' Muntz, Briggs Cunningham and Brooks Stevens conceived the Muntz Jet, Cunningham and Excalibur J. The trend was strong enough for General Motors to enter the field with a Chevrolet sports car.

At this point, and indeed almost to the start of Corvette production, there was no definite commitment to using glass-reinforced-plastic (GRP) instead of conventional steel or (heaven forbid!) aluminum for the sports car's bodywork. In the end, of course, Chevrolet would hail the Corvette body as a wonder of the age; but, in fact, GRP and similar materials had been considered by motor manufacturers for at least 15 years.

The impetus for an alternative body material we may credit to Henry Ford who, in 1929, asked a group of young researchers from his trade-school laboratory to come up with an industry outlet for farm products. Two years later, after reading *The Soybean*, by C. V. Piper and W. J. Morse, Ford became fascinated by this humble vegetable, ordering his men to 'throw everything you are working on out' and tackle the soybean as a car component. The lab used the soybean's yield of phenolformaldehyde to produce a reinforced plastic by mixing it with wood fibers, then pressing it into plastic body panels.

Ford brought acreage in Dearborn to 'grow enough soybeans for a million cars', and, albeit for entirely different reasons, by 1970 it was second only to wheat among American cash crops. Although it never worked out quite as Ford intended, it did lead to fibrous glovebox doors and tractor seats, fiber-based knobs and fascia trim – even a plastic bootlid for Henry's personal 1941 Ford coupe, which he demonstrated widely.

Ultimately, Ford built a plastic experimental car with surface panels made of phenolic resin and wood-fiber pulp, mixed and strengthened with flax, hemp and raimi, and shaped against a mesh screen while the mix was still in solution. The body was 30 per cent lighter than an identical steel body. Although he didn't know it then, Henry Ford was pioneering the manufacturing technique of glass-reinforced plastic automobile bodies.

General Motors' first plastic research program had begun in 1938, in conjunction with what is now Owens-Corning. Although GM did learn how to use plastic for interior bits like handles, knobs and dashboard trim, its research into an all-plastic car produced nothing worth recording. The real breakthrough came from a boat builder, Glasspar Inc.

Glasspar was founded in 1950 by Bill Tritt, Otto Baeyer, Jerry Niger and financier Louis Solomon to produce vast quantities of small boat hulls out of glass-reinforced plastic, but they quickly became involved in car bodies as well. A year before the Glasspar venture, Tritt had experimented in building a car bodied in glass-reinforced plastic.

During the war, research had brought GRP to a very practical state of refinement. It was used to provide various protective structural coverings over radar and other delicate equipment, covers which could withstand extreme ranges of temperature and rough use. GRP began to be used by car designers like Tritt and Howard Darrin as early as 1946; they found the material easy to mold, exceptionally strong yet light, with good impact resistance and high-luster quality when painted.

Darrin built a full-size, GRP-bodied convertible for Kaiser-Frazer, and later convinced that

firm to produce the GRP Kaiser Darrin; Tritt brought his ideas to Glasspar. One of his early efforts was a streamlined Willys Jeep called the Brooks Boxer, shown at the Los Angeles Motorama in late 1951.

Reaction to the Boxer was encouraging, so Tritt interested US Rubber's Naugatauck Chemical Division (supplier of GRP raw materials) in helping to finance Glasspar's auto body research. This was a key development in the GRP, and Corvette, story.

In early 1952, Glasspar announced a new, Tritt-designed roadster, very low and sleek, available in kit form for various production chassis of around 100 inches in wheelbase. By the end of the year, a wide variety of GRP-bodied sports-car conversions were announced. These included Ralph Roberts's Skorpion, at $460, designed for the Crosley chassis, and the Super Skorpion, a more sophisticated body for Crosley, Renault 4CV and Morris Minor chassis, costing $640. The Testaguzza Body Company of Ogden, Michigan, produced a $1000 body called La Sietta for longer-chassis Chevrolets; Eric Irwin offered the Lancer, which would fit any wheelbase from 100 to 110 inches. Vale Wright of Berkeley, California, had a GRP body for the MG TD – as did Atlas Fiber-Glass, whose version looked like a Cisitalia coupé and sold for $685. Of all these early efforts, General Motors Engineering took careful note.

It was Glasspar, however, who finally proved glass-reinforced plastic's practicality by producing the first fiberglass sports car readily available off a showroom floor: the Woodill Wildfire. This project, by a Californian Willys dealer named (of course) Woody Woodill, used a 101-inch wheelbase and a 90 bhp F-head Willys six coupled to a three-speed overdrive transmission. Fully assembled, it sold for $2900 (later raised to $3275), and weighed only 1620lb at the kerb. Woodill signed up a number of Willys dealers to market the car, and sold from 200 to 300 Wildfires from 1952 through 1958, some with Ford or Mercury V8 engines. Most, Woodills, however, were sold in kit form.

The Wildfire was a fine test-case for Glasspar's methods, which were progressively polished and refined. Through it they learned how to compensate for the two to three per cent shrinkage that occurs in the curing of GRP after the final mold is formed. The Wildfire also showed Glasspar how to eliminate a serious wear problem at the metal attachment points: angle-iron brackets were bonded directly to the body, covered with three layers of GRP and painted with several coats of polyester resin. Small screws, which easily worked loose in GRP bodies, were anchored with rubber grommets. The Wildfire project lay behind Glasspar's early and continuing success in the business, and formed the basic pool of technical know-how that made the Corvette possible.

GRP was a new material in those days, with great cost-saving potential on a low-volume model such as GM contemplated, since the essential dies were much less expensive than steel ones. One remaining doubt concerned GRP's strength, but Chevrolet engineers examining Glasspar boats and Wildfire car bodies were soon convinced that GRP would hold up. When a prototype Corvette was accidentally rolled on the proving grounds, the driver escaping unscathed and the major body components surviving intact, GM management was satisfied with GRP — which was soon nicknamed fiberglass (US) or glassfibre (UK); 'Fibreglass', incidentally, is a manufacturer's registered trademark.

Such decisions are much more complicated nowadays but this, remember, was the 1950s. Early fiberglass burned easily so today's safety lobby would have had a field day with it. On the other hand, Chevrolet soon recognized the problem and took fire-proofing measures which the fiberglass industry quickly adopted.

Chevrolet's decision to use fiberglass for its sports car wasn't a foregone conclusion, although it certainly allowed the first showcar to be built in

time; but GM still wavered. According to engineer Ellis Premo, 'we were actually concentrating on a steel body utilizing Kirksite tooling for the projected production of 10 000 units for the 1954 model year'. Kirksite dies are cheaper than conventional dies but do not last as long, nor would they have held up over the production of 10 000 units — not that Chevrolet managed to sell that many of the early Corvettes.

Simultaneously with GM's investigation of body materials, the corporation's formidable design team had been developing the new car's styling. Since 1927, when he had arrived at Cadillac to conjure up the magnificent original LaSalle, Harley J. Earl had directed the design of all GM cars. A pioneer of the automotive design profession, Earl maintained a crack team of young designers in what he called the Art and Colour Studio, which later became GM Styling Staff. Under Earl, GM styling led the industry for 30 years, until it was temporarily eclipsed by Virgil Exner and Chrysler.

Harley Earl was a leading advocate of a GM sports car from the time it was first mooted. Initially, he took a leaf from the MG book by proposing a classic British formula: a special two-seat body hung around production components and a tuned production engine selling for as little as $1800. But gradually plans evolved into something more elaborate. The Corvette design work was codenamed 'Project Opel' — the name of GM's German subsidiary serving as a disguise.

The man who led Earl to his final decision about the production car's shape was a young graduate of Cal Tech, Robert J. McLean, whose conception seemed a long shot: a long-hood/short-deck two-seater with a near-50/50 weight distribution. McLean achieved these seemingly contradictory characteristics by commencing his design from the set-point of the rear axle, rather than the engine and front wheels as usual. He also specified a very wide track: 59 inches front, 57 rear — much wider, for example, than the XK120. Details like the toothy oval grille, nerf-style bumpers, rounded fuselage and wrap-around one-piece windshield were largely derived from Harley Earl's Buick XP-300 showcar, a favorite of the Art and Colour Studio.

The Corvette's inset headlamps with wire-mesh stone guards, 'lollipop' tail-lights and dummy knock-off wheel covers, were influenced respectively by contemporary sports-car practice, contemporary Harley Earl practice and a combination of the two. The 'first generation' 1953–5 Vette was forever criticized for those dummy knock-offs, and the 'shadow-box' arrangement for the rear license plate on the trunklid (surely the latter was nothing more than the streamlined headlamp cover in reverse?).

Perennial critics of Corvettes, especially of this first generation, never seem to think about what it took for such a car to be considered by a company the size of General Motors. They always point to the inevitable compromises — but such were essential if the Corvette was to earn its place in production. At GM a sports car required considerably more sales than a comparable model would at, say, Jaguar.

We should also remember that its ultimate character — a genuine dual-purpose, raceable sports car — had not yet been established. General Motors wanted the car to achieve decent sales volume, yet every survey GM made showed that true sports cars held about seven-tenths of one per cent of the American market. Its appeal had to be broader. Equally important to GM was the *idea* of a sports car — the sheer presence and élan a Corvette would bring to staid Chevrolet sales floors. If anything, this publicity value was even more important than total sales. If along the way Chevrolet could pick up a few thousand sales as a *boulevardier*, all the better.

While Harley Earl's original $1800 target eventually came to be only about half the Corvette's retail price, enormous efforts still had to be made to keep the overheads down. This would show on announcement in such cost-cutting equipment as side curtains — previously

anathema to Detroit. But production engineers had to grapple with 'prodifying' measures even more basic, concerning the chassis and drivetrain. Most of the running gear, GM decreed, would have to come from existing parts bins. What's more, the job was assigned to Chevrolet Division, so they would have to be Chevrolet parts and, among other things, Chevy lacked a V8.

One expense was unavoidable: the Corvette chassis had to be designed from scratch. Contemporary two-seat showcars used mere shortened production-car chassis; that was impossible with the Corvette because of Bob McLean's far-back engine position. Front suspension bits and pieces were on hand, but the rear end was unique, even revolutionary, at least for Chevrolet. The Division had traditionally used torque-tube drive; the Corvette adopted Hotchkiss (open) drive, and located the rear leaf springs outboard of the main frame rails for added stability, a feature duly extended to 1955 Chevrolet passenger cars.

The engine was a problem. At that time the only really high-output engines in Detroit were V8s, and only three GM divisions — Cadillac, Buick and Oldsmobile — had them. Arguably the only one that might have fitted was the small 5-litre Oldsmobile Rocket but Chevrolet never considered borrowing the Olds engine. This was not so much out of refusal to cross-pollinate (Chevy engines duly powered Oldsmobiles much later, to the embarrassment of dealers), but because Chevrolet *did* have a V8 coming. The only sensible immediate possibility if the Corvette was to debut in 1953, was the Chevrolet Blue Flame six. Yet applying this 108bhp 3.8-liter trundler to the Corvette seemed like trying to charcoal-broil a steak over a pilot light.

Enter Ed Cole, which meant things were going to get better in a hurry. Chevrolet chief engineer Edward Nicholas Cole had been broken in at Cadillac in 1933, after graduating from the GM Institute. During the war he had designed light tanks and military vehicles; afterwards he'd worked on rear-engine prototypes for both Cadillac and Chevrolet, including the ill-starred Cadet small car which GM shelved in the big-car-happy 1940s. Cole had also helped John Gordon to develop the fine overhead-valve Cadillac V8 of 1949. He had been brought into Chevrolet (from a 30-month stint managing the Cadillac Cleveland plant) to produce a similar engine for GM's bread-and-butter division. To Cole, the Corvette was a side issue, even if an exciting one. It needed an engine, the V8 wasn't ready, so he would modify the six.

Cole told the author that the Corvette six 'was really just another leaf out of the MG book', referring to the British concept of a 'cooking' version of a production-line engine for sports-car applications. 'It was a good, reliable unit, with plenty of potential,' Cole continued. 'No one had simply tried to do anything with it before — there was no need.' Until the Corvette, Chevrolet's long reign as 'USA No. 1' was based entirely on inexpensive, conventional and very dull family transport.

On becoming chief engineer, Cole had increased Chevrolet's engineering staff from 850 to 2900, and it was this capable team that transformed the Blue Flame six, bestowing it with a high-lift/long-duration camshaft, solid valve-lifters, dual valve springs to cope with higher rpm, a modified head with 8:1 compression (up from 7.5:1), improved coolant flow and a vastly improved induction system. Instead of the single, small carburetor of the Chevy passenger car, the Corvette engine received triple Carter type YH sidedraft carbs on an aluminum intake manifold. Linkage was simultaneous, not progressive: all three carbs operated at the same time, each feeding two cylinders. At the other end of the system, dual exhausts assured low restriction and a rorty sound. The snarl of a six-cylinder Corvette, accelerating hard, is one of its most pleasant characteristics. One minor design feature mandated by the low hood was a redesigned rocker-arm cover which, however, was not chromed or finned, and looked very much like the ordinary

passenger-car rocker cover apart from reading 'Blue Flame Special'.

The result of all this work was an impressive forty per cent improvement in power: 150bhp at 4500rpm (and it could rev higher than that). It is worth noting that the only other 'performance six' in America — the 1953 Hudson Hornet, US stock-car champion for 1952–4 — required 308 cubic inches (5 liters) to develop 145bhp. Curiously, in the American old-car hobby, the Hornet gets constant praise as the 'hot six' of the period, everyone forgetting that the Corvette had it beat in bhp per liter.

'With transmissions as well as engines,' Ed Cole said when explaining why his sports car had an automatic transmission, 'we simply didn't have anything else. I know people think it's very funny, the thought of mighty General Motors, stuck for a transmission. But it's true. This whole job was a peripheral, shoestring project. You don't design a competent four-speed with the time and money we had. Our three-speed wouldn't stand up to the power the Corvette engine developed. Tests showed Powerglide would.' Cole's points are well taken. Remember, even cars like Jaguar were using Moss gearboxes with primitive synchromesh any kid with a fast arm could beat and in any case, the four-speed was unknown in America in 1953.

There was no choice: for the nonce, it was Powerglide or forget it. Even with Powerglide, it must be noted, the typical six-cylinder Corvette would be 0–60mph in 11 seconds and achieve 105mph, which was hardly bad.

With these bits and pieces in his hands, Ed Cole met Harley Earl to see what Styling had wrought. 'He literally jumped up and down,' wrote Karl Ludvigsen. Ed promised to stick with Harley through thick and thin, until the car they'd jointly crafted was scheduled for production. A few weeks later, in mid 1952, a full-size plaster model was presented to GM president Harlow Curtice and Chevrolet Division general manager Tom Keating. Earl pointed out the Vette's double-barreled mission: to sell well on its own, but moreover to add needed glamor and allure to the Chevrolet showroom. Harley was a very persuasive man. Curtice and Keating agreed to test-announce the car at the GM Motorama, that legendary convocation of glitz, girls and gladioli, planned for the New York Waldorf-Astoria in January 1953. Project Opel was in the bag!

As Ed Cole remembered, 'that was tantamount to a go for production, and in fact production was never in doubt from that point on. The Polo-White prototype, prepared for the Motorama as experimental project EX-122, was one of the hits of the show, as everybody knew it would be. Harley Earl mingled with the crowd, said to have totaled four million, picking up their reactions to his showcars; all he heard about the Corvette were questions. Mainly, they were 'How much?' and 'When?'.

The answer to the first question proved to be: $3513, inclusive of Powerglide automatic, Delco signal-seeking radio, 5000rpm tachometer, with a counter for total engine revolutions, and a powerful recirculating hot-water heater. The answer to the second question was more problematic.

The pioneering nature of GRP bodywork was a time-consuming blockade to immediate production. Chevrolet needed to know a lot more about high-volume production, including curing properties, stress ability and final finish techniques for this new body material. It took almost six months before Corvette production began, at an auxiliary building next to the Chevrolet plant in Flint, Michigan, on 30 June 1953. Even with that delay it was only about a year since the original model had been shown to Curtice and Keating by Harley Earl and his styling staff.

Largely handmade, and therefore differing from car to car in precise detail, the 1953 Corvettes were finished in Polo White, with Sportsman Red and White interiors and black folding tops. All were equipped with 6.70 × 15 white sidewall four-ply tires and full wheel covers. The

late Sam Folz, a prominent Corvette authority and friend, listed for this writer a number of obvious differences between these production cars and the Motorama showcar. The production cars had fewer chrome-plated engine parts, no fan shroud, no 'Corvette' nameplate on hood and trunk, manual (not hydraulic) door/top opening, no exterior door push-buttons, a full length bright-metal body molding, white rather than chrome-plated internal door knobs, no extra dummy dashboard knobs (the showcar had two, on the right), windshield-end and drip-molding seals, no upper front fender scoops, wide headlamp bezels, smaller wheel-cover spinners, a vinyl-covered upper dash edge and a manual choke. Automatic chokes had proved impossible, since the three carburetors warmed up at different rates; a manual choke was not the whole solution, but at least it had the benefit of being controllable.

With the Corvette in production, sort of, general manager Tom Keating made a decision to produce only 300 cars for the balance of the '53 model year and to evaluate them carefully before launching into serious volume for '54. It was a decision typical of the Chevrolet of that time, characteristically cautious — and eminently disastrous. The first few cars went to Chevy engineers, the rest to handpicked owners: GM executives, film stars, sports celebrities and the like. The general public didn't have a chance and most of the glut of initial customers simply went away mad. By 1954, when Keating was ready to sell, they'd already bought a big Detroit convertible, or a Jaguar. As any market analyst worth his salt should have pointed out, the considerably quicker Jaguar XK120 roadster sold for $3345 — $168 less than the Corvette. As a result, by the end of 1953, the Corvette's future was in serious jeopardy.

Which was unfortunate, for the 1954 Corvette was free of all hand assembly, perfected in detail, readily available — and cheaper. Reacting to the tall list price of the '53 (and able to make

ZORA ARKUS-DUNTOV

Zora retired in 1974 after almost two decades as the Corvette's engineering Godfather. He wasn't called Mr Corvette for nothing; without him, it is impossible to imagine the early cars developing as they did or even existing.

Born in Belgium, Arkus-Duntov brought both academic training as an engineer and hands-on experience to Chevrolet. The experience came at Allard in England, a company perhaps the total opposite of Chevrolet, but pursuing a remarkably similar line of building rapid sports cars from production-car components. In 1953, having already moved to America to join Fairchild Aviation, Duntov sent a paper on high-performance engines to Chevy chief engineer Ed Cole. After considerable bargaining over salary and benefits, Cole hired him. He was probably the first European performance engineer hired by General Motors, but certainly the first one Chevrolet had seen!

Duntov found the 1953 Corvette about as close to his ideas of a sports car as the horse-drawn carriage is to the motor car. It had four wheels and it was driveable, but resemblances ended there. Neither did he pay much attention to the rules, thankfully. His assignment was to improve performance of the standard Chevy, but before long he was working almost entirely on Corvettes. That they let him get away with it is indicative of the respect they had for him (and of Ed Cole's dominance of the engineering establishment).

If Chevy gave out academy awards, Zora would have a mantel full. His 'Duntov cam' turned the original Corvette small-block from a very nice, mild-mannered V8 into a tiger. He virtually invented the mid-engined Q-Corvette, and used his racing experience with everything from the Sebring SS to stock models to design the all new, state-of-the-art suspension for the 1963 Sting Ray. He fought everybody, from top management and Bill Mitchell to the ad agency and sales departments, on behalf of an uncompromising sports car. Most times he won, even in the early '70s, when everyone thought the whole *idea* of the Corvette was doomed by government edicts and the sudden shortage of petroleum. He kept winning after retirement, developing the Duntov-Corvette conversion of the relatively staid '75 coupe into a total-performance roadster.

He had one main regret: that he reached GM's mandatory retirement age before he could finally 'sell' the mid-engine concept to GM. He liked the current product, but thought it had too many compromises, the digital instruments in particular! 'The speedometer and tach should have round faces to show where you have been and where you are going. Instantaneous readouts have no place in a sports car,' he commented. One wishes he was still in there swinging. . . .

economies once production was under way in earnest), Chevrolet drastically lowered the base price, to $2774. This was somewhat misleading, since Powerglide was now a $178 'option' (mandatory, since there was no other transmission) — as were the radio, heater and whitewalls, which had come as standard on the $3513 model. Adding up these costs, along with miscellany like directional signals, parking-brake alarm, courtesy lights and shieldsquirt, brought the tab to $3254: still a few hundred less than the original.

The improvements wrought in the '54 went beyond the lower price. Most important, saleswise, there was now a choice of color: while most Vettes came in Polo White, buyers could opt for Pennant Blue (sixteen per cent) or Sportsman Red (four per cent); and about a half-dozen were painted black with red interiors. Metallic bronze and green were listed in certain paint bulletins, and some collectors claim to have seen original cars in these colors. Another '54 change saw the previous black convertible top and top irons changed to tan. Many other useful physical changes were made, plus one small mechanical one: a new camshaft was fitted, to raise engine output to 155bhp, although this was not announced until 1955.

The problem, of course, was that customers had now become very scarce. Despite a probable capacity of 10 000 units, Chevrolet built only 3640 '54 Corvettes and, as the '55 model year began, about 1500 of those were still unsold. The car was quite plainly *not* profitable. Nor was the Corvette's other main purpose, its role as an image-maker, as important as it had been. In Detroit in the '50s, what was new one day was old hat the next. Inevitably, GM management began to have second thoughts about continuing the Corvette beyond 1955.

Harley Earl had proposed a substantial '55 facelift, with a functional air scoop, dummy side-panel louvres, an egg-crate grille similar to that of the '55 Chevy passenger cars and a new tail end free of the lollipop tail-lamps. But with sales

dismal, he could find no higher-ups willing to back it, and the Corvette entered 1955 little changed, showing every outward sign that this would be its final year. Early in production, Harvest Gold (with green trim and top) replaced Pennant Blue as a paint scheme, and Gypsy Red replaced Sportsman Red. The '55 bodies were smoother and thinner in section than before, and workmanship, improved in 1954, improved again.

Late in the year a close-ratio, three-speed stickshift option to the Powerglide automatic finally appeared, but few cars had it. Substantially, then, the '55 was unchanged, except for one crucial factor: all but six '55s had Chevrolet's hot new V8.

Designed under Ed Cole's direction, this powerful, efficient 'small-block' (265cu in, 4.3-liter) V8 was an outstanding powerplant, the engine Cole had been brought to Chevrolet to create. Of course, it immediately transformed the image and feel of the big Chevy passenger cars, which fortuitously were restyled at the same time; it also — incidentally — transformed the Corvette. Zero to 60, formerly done in 11 seconds with the six, now took between 8 and 9; the standing-start quarter-mile, which used to require 19 seconds, now took 16.5. The Vette's top speed was up 15mph, now approaching 120, yet most road tests reported *improved* fuel mileage compared with the six. *Road & Track* averaged just over 20 miles per gallon (16mpg Imperial), 2–3 mpg better! It seemed like the best of all possible worlds.

The V8 delivered 162bhp in standard passenger-car form, but was modified to produce 195bhp at 5000rpm in the Corvette. Other appropriate changes included a reversion to automatic choke (the complicated triple carbs had given way to a single Carter four-barrel), a 6000rpm rev counter, a 12-volt electrical system (sixes retained the 6-volt) and the elimination of the Powerglide vacuum modulator. The kickdown was now governed solely by speed and throttle position. There was no change in axle ratio, although the few late '55s fitted with the three-speed manual gearbox had a slightly lower ratio, and were commensurately faster, sprinting from 0–60 in 8 seconds flat.

The V8 improved the Corvette in a major way, but to many potential buyers in 1955 it still appeared deficient. It was, after all, still fairly pricey; the base price of the V8 was close to $3000. That was a fair amount of money in those days although, factored for inflation ($11 000), it doesn't seem like a lot today. But dealers were reporting buyer resistance to certain spartan characteristics of the Corvette which had been there since the beginning: the handle-less doors, the bodywork of an unfamiliar material and, above all, the side curtains in lieu of roll-up windows.

The people walking into Chevrolet dealerships were not, after all, Triumph and Austin-Healey buyers, and they did not expect this peculiar alternative to the convenient window crank. Besides, by 1955, Ford had their new Thunderbird, which had none of the Corvette's peculiarities. Whereas Chevrolet would only manage to sell a grand total of 668 Corvette V8s and a half-dozen sixes in 1955, the T-bird sold at the enviable rate of 1400 a month. Ford now had what Chevrolet had wanted, both a two-seat image maker and a decent seller. And that, of all things, is what actually saved the Corvette.

It is hard to describe just how seriously Ford and Chevrolet took their '50s rivalry. Every fall, the two would issue claims and counter-claims over who had sold the most cars. Attempting to finish first in 1953, Henry Ford II had shipped thousands of cars to dealers who had not ordered them, telling them to sell 'em or die. Chevy reacted in kind, and the losers, ironically, were Chrysler and the small independents. Whatever Ford did, Chevrolet had to do better, and *vice versa*.

Zora Arkus-Duntov, the brilliant German whose name will for ever be linked with Corvette's, remembered: 'There were conversations. . . about the Corvette being dropped. Then the Thunderbird came out and all of a sudden GM was keeping the Corvette. I think that Ford brought out the competitive spirit in Ed Cole'. Cole himself was more conservative, telling this writer: 'It was a broad-based decision in which many things figured, but you'd not be wrong to think the Thunderbird had a profound influence'. Asked whether the Corvette would have managed to survive without the presence of the Thunderbird, Cole replied: 'That would have tilted the odds against it'.

Corvette would live to fight another day, and we cannot help but ponder the ironies. Unheard of in Detroit for 30 years, the sports car got into production in response to American tastes shaped over 3000 miles away in Britain. Incomprehensibly, for Detroit, it was built of something other than steel. Incredibly, for a Chevrolet, it didn't sell. And unbelievably, for General Motors, its bacon was saved by a Ford.

Best Vettes

1954 Six

Perverse choice? Everyone knows the original 1953 model is the rarest and most desirable of first-generation Corvettes, and that the 1955 V8 had the legs of its predecessors. Reliable price guides show both of these leading the in-between 1954 model by about ten per cent. Why then do we single out the '54 Vette as the best of the lot? Partly for some of the above reasons, and partly for outside factors.

Today, as in its own time, the 1954 Corvette is the most readily available of the early cars. For today's collector, that means the choice of car is relatively broader and the chances of getting a nice example for less money considerably better. Nor does the 1954 seem much less desirable as an investment, since its value has galloped along with the other Corvettes, and will continue to produce handsome returns.

Intrinsically, the '54 has many merits compared with the virtually hand-made '53s. All '54s were built in the new St Louis plant, with greater attention to fit and finish, a better paint job and better workmanship. At least some were available in Pennant Blue, Sportsman Red and black, as well as the original Polo White. Tops were tan instead of black, and tan seems to contrast handsomely with the exterior colours.

Numerous small improvements combined to make the '54 a pleasanter package all round: the old, two-handle hood latch was replaced by a more manageable single-handle mechanism on all but the first 300-odd '54s; the choke control was relocated from right to left under the steering column, switching position with the wiper switch and eliminating the problem of having to reach across or through the steering wheel to operate the choke with the left hand while turning the ignition key with the right; weather sealing was considerably improved. Beginning with serial number 3600, top irons were redesigned with a dogleg shape that allowed them to disappear between the body and the seatback, rather than poke through slots in the chrome moldings behind the seats, as in the '53 model.

Under the bonnet, the wiring harness was tidier, with more plastic-insulated wire replacing the fabric type, and the engine had a new rocker-arm cover, often attractively chrome-plated. Most important was the engine itself: the highest developed form of Blue Flame six, which has been grossly underrated.

Best Vettes

There are plenty of Corvette V8s to suit every taste in succeeding generations; this generation was the only one designed for and available with Ed Cole's performance six. Comparisons are revealing:

Year	Model	Liters	Bhp @ Rpm	Bhp/Liter
1954	Corvette	3.87	155 @ 4200	40.1
1954	Hudson Hornet	5.05	160 @ 3800	31.7
1954	Jaguar XK120	3.44	160 @ 5200	46.5

Considering that the Hudson Hornet was America's stock-car racing champion, and that Jaguar's great twin-cam six cylinder won laurels at Le Mans, the Corvette engine comes off very well indeed. Adding the fact that Ed Cole's modifications delivered this level of performance without sacrificing smoothness or reliability, we can only conclude that this was one of the best-engineered performance sixes of the early post-war years. Wrapped in Harley Earl's svelte bodywork, it adds up to a very desirable Corvette.

Best Yettes

1954 CORVETTE SPECIFICATION

ENGINE

Type	In-line 'Blue Flame' six cylinder with cast-iron block and heads
Bore	3.56in
Stroke	3.95in
Displacement	235.5cu in
Compression ratio	8.0:1
Valve gear	Two in-line valves per cylinder operated by single block mounted camshaft, pushrods and rockers
Fuel system	Three Carter sidedraft carburetors
Maximum power	155bhp at 4200rpm
Maximum torque	233lb ft at 2400rpm

TRANSMISSION

Type	Two-speed Powerglide automatic with torque convertor
Ratios	1st 3.83:1 2nd 1.0:1
Rear axle ratio	3.55:1
Body/Chassis	Two seat fibreglass convertible body on box-section steel X frame

SUSPENSION

Front	Independent with upper and lower wishbones, coil springs, tubular hydraulic shock absorbers and anti-roll bar
Rear	Non independent with live axle, longitudinal leaf springs and telescopic shock absorbers
Steering	Saginaw worm and sector
Brakes	Drums front and rear, 11in dia, 154.5sq in swept area

1954 CORVETTE SPECIFICATION
continued

DIMENSIONS AND WEIGHT

Length	167.0in
Wheelbase	102.0in
Width	72.2in
Track	57.0in front
	59.0in rear
Height	51.3in
Weight	2850lb

PERFORMANCE

0—30mph	3.7secs
0—40mph	5.3secs
0—50mph	7.7secs
0—60mph	11.0secs

Standing quarter miles 17.9secs

Top speed 107mph

Fuel consumption 16mpg

PAGE 33 Recessed headlamps with protective wire mesh grille were a feature of the first Corvette generation.

PAGES 34/45 Corvettes out in force in a Chevrolet public relations exercise staged with a backdrop of San Francisco's Golden Gate bridge. Why the demonstration? Sales were slow and interest had to be created.

PAGES 36/37 By 1961 a certain amount of the excessive chrome of the '50s had gone — the headlamp surrounds, for example, are painted and the grille is far less clumsy.

ABOVE There had to be a good reason why the Motorama fastback coupe proposed as a production car for 1955 never materialized, because its lines are near enough perfect.

PAGES 38/39 & FACING PAGE The 1960 model year was notable in being the first in which annual sales broke 10 000. It was also the third year in which Rochester fuel injection had been offered, giving either 275 or 315bhp, which was enough to power the car to 60mph in under 8 seconds and cover the standing quarter in under 16 secs. The 150mph shown on the speedo was only a trifle optimistic, the true maximum being near 140mph.

PAGES 43/44 And here is that reason. The unsold convertibles made Chevrolet management cautious. This time it's a Corvette display in the east, not in Detroit as you might suspect but in Chicago, along Lake Shore Drive to be precise. The display doesn't seem to have grabbed the attention of the passing sedan drivers, however.

PREVIOUS SPREAD Even the youngest of the first generation Corvettes is now well over thirty years old, but the car still looks less old-fashioned than the model's attire, a ghostly echo of the '40s.

ABOVE The first Corvette engine was derived from an existing Chevrolet design but modified, tuned and fitted with treble Carter sidedrafts by Zora Arkus-Duntov to produce 150bhp at 4200rpm from its 235cu in. That was enough to give the first Corvettes their amazing 106mph performance.

FACING PAGE Hardtops came with the '53 and '54 model years . . . but not the '55. That wasn't such a hardship, however, as the aftermarket had stepped in by this time.

ABOVE The license plate tells you it's a '58, but if that wasn't there the nine-tooth grille would be the proof, as would the louvered hood. Engine size was 283cu in, the V8 being available with outputs from 230 to 290bhp (with fuel injection).

HITTING
ITS
STRIDE

1956 – 1962

ACHIEVING GM's benevolent blessing for the Corvette's continuance was something of a victory for the enthusiast types at Chevrolet Division, and they were confident of their car and its cause. To outsiders it may have looked like the heat was on to succeed or die in 1956, but the engineers, designers and managers who conceived the new model had no doubts about its success. By the end of the '50s they were vindicated: the '56 Corvette equalled the sales of the '54; the '57 Corvette doubled that figure and the '58 tripled it (despite a very grim year for the American industry as a whole). In 1960, Corvette sales exceeded 10 000, and have done so ever since. It is significant that such a sales level was entirely acceptable to GM, whereas Ford had disdained the 15 000 average annual sales of the two-seat Thunderbird. Comparing the two cars helps explain the reason for such markedly different attitudes, but first, let us trace the second-generation Corvette to its roots.

Stylistically, the 1956–62 Corvette generation was very much the work of Harley Earl. The '56 model was rooted in Earl's contemporary Motor-ama showcars, the Biscayne and LaSalle II, which also influenced the styling of big Chevrolet passenger models. They were vintage-Earl, with large, vertical-tooth grilles, inboard headlamps, fully-radiused wheel openings, acres of glass and a concave scoop breaking up the body sides. This last was one of Earl's favorite styling ploys, harking back to his years as a custom coachbuilder before the war. The 'cove' was strongly emphasised with a contrasting color – Harley even proposed filling it with another of his preferred finishes, brushed aluminum. That didn't happen on production Corvettes but not through want of trying.

The front end, while clearly related to the 1953–5 design, was more functional. Although the basic grille design was unaltered, the headlamps had been moved into conventional positions at the tips of the fenders, and the stoneguard meshwork of the first generation vanished. The tail end was nicely rounded, losing all trace of 'lollipop' tail-lamps: these were now modest round lights mounted high on the fenders which were scooped to repeat the side-cove theme.

Exhaust gases exited through the rear bumper guards; this was a common '50s practice but not a very practical one since it led to discoloration of the bright metal. Overall, the 1956 Corvette looked like a cross between a Mercedes-Benz 300SL and a softly rounded two-seater from Turin; compared with its predecessor, it seemed neat, functional and far more serious. The only components that seemed contrived were the non-functional scoops mounted near the cowl on the front fenders and the persistent feature of wheel-covers with dummy knock-off hubs.

Eliminating in one swoop the whines of dealers and the buying public, side curtains were replaced by proper roll-up windows (there was even a power-lift option) and outside door handles were fitted. Duplicating an idea seen on the Thunderbird (but which seems first to have appeared on the 1954 Triumph TR2), there appeared a lift-off hardtop with a large expanse of glass. Its design was almost unchanged from the 1954 GM Motorama prototype.

Mechanically, the V8 was obviously the way to go on a performance car and the six-cylinder engine was discarded. Although the V8 was unchanged in displacement, an increase in compression ratio brought it up to 210bhp at 5200rpm with the usual four-barrel carburetor. Special camshafts, a cast-aluminum intake manifold and twin four-barrels were available, which increased output to 225 and 240bhp. There was still no four-speed transmission; a heavy-duty three-speed manual gearbox was standard, relegating Powerglide to an option. This underlined the decision to pursue the sports-car rather than the luxury-car route, a major difference between the 1956 Corvette and 1956 Thunderbird.

By the time the two cars appeared, Ford had already decided to enlarge the T-bird to a four-seater by 1958. Although this fact was not public knowledge in 1956, the diverging philosophy of the two cars was obvious.

Dimensionally, the pair rode on a 102-inch wheelbase, but the Thunderbird was 18 inches longer overall and 6 inches wider. Although the Ford's engine was somewhat larger, both cars developed almost the same horsepower, but there the similarities ended. The Thunderbird was designed for a soft ride, while the Corvette, engineered by people like Cole and Zora Arkus-Duntov, rode more like a sports car, transmitting tire and road noise to the driver. Inevitably, the Corvette handled better, while the T-bird plowed in tight corners and had a tendency to float over dips and bumps. The Corvette's manual steering was more precise than the T-bird's; power steering reduced the turns lock-to-lock but diminished road feel. Off the line, despite the Ford weighing about 300lb more, the cars were equals: 0–60 took about 10–12 seconds (depending on transmission and axle ratios); the quarter-mile 17–18 seconds at 75–78mph; and both cars returned about 13mpg.

'The Thunderbird is pretty much what Ford claims it is – a "personal car", suitable for the bachelor, for the young or "young in heart" couple, or for the husband or wife as a second car,' said *Motor Trend* in a 1956 comparison test. 'The Corvette is less of a personal car and closer to being, or easily becoming, a sports car. The sales philosophy of Chevrolet seems to have been more to compete with the foreign sports-car market – at least until the Thunderbird came along. Now it appears that they're trying to split down the middle by providing more highway comfort for the average person and/or the ability to make the car into a sports car by the addition of the modification kit (finned brakes, limited-slip differential, disc brakes, and heavy-duty springs). Which one for you? Within $2.60, you can have your choice.' Incredibly, the *MT* test cars were priced only $2.60 apart.

Just how far apart the two rivals were, even then, was finally proven on the race tracks. While the two-seat Thunderbirds were occasionally raced, mainly in regional Sports Car Club of America (SCCA) events, they rarely performed with distinction. In contrast, Dr Richard Thompson, a dentist from Washington DC, won the class C-Production SCCA championship in 1956. Earlier, Duntov himself, driving a modified '56, set a record 105.583mph for the flying mile at Daytona Beach, Florida. A few weeks later, at the Daytona Speed Weeks of January 1956, Betty Skelton set an American sports-car speed record, and John Fitch took best-in-class for modified sports cars in the standing mile, at a speed of 145.543mph. True, a very carefully prepared Thunderbird, entered by tuning wizard Pete DePaolo and driven by Chuck Daigh, beat the Corvettes in the 'production' standing mile — but this was one of the few times, in head-to-head competition, that the Ford prevailed. Of course, there was no Ford competition at all after the 'Bird went to its larger, four-seat configuration in 1958.

Part of the success of these early Vettes was owed to the serious interest taken in the car by Chevrolet, notably Duntov himself. The aforementioned 'Duntov cam' was part of the reason for these winning efforts, as was Duntov's high-compression cylinder heads, which raised power on modified 265 V8s close to 1bhp per cubic inch.

How did Duntov get away with all this time and expenditure on what remained a highly peripheral product? The answer, as Zora explained in later years, was that, peripheral or not, the Corvette was gaining good publicity, earning GM in general and Chevrolet in particular a reputation for performance at the very height of the performance craze in America. The result was increased floor traffic at Chevy dealerships bringing more sales of conventional Chevy cars. Somehow, the Corvette was succeeding where other limited-edition publicity stunts (such as the Continental Mark II, Cadillac Eldorado Brougham, Packard Caribbean, Nash-Healey, Hudson Italia and Kaiser Darrin) failed. This endeared the Corvette to hard-bitten managers who didn't know the first thing about sports cars. Duntov played his hand well.

The most exciting racing in 1956 was done at the Sebring Twelve Hours in Florida, where a Fitch team of four Corvettes with oversize fuel tanks, driving lights and Halibrand mag wheels were set to do battle in April. Three of these were 255bhp production Corvettes with Duntov mods; a fourth, entered in the prototype class, had been bored out to 5 liters and fitted with a ZF four-speed gearbox.

Three of the four Corvettes finished — 'a magnificent tribute to the cars' overall competitive record', as Chevrolet put it. The modified car and one of the production models finished fifteenth and ninth overall and won their respective classes. A third, the owner's personal car, which had received no special preparation and ran with such equipment as radio, heater and power top, was still in the race at the end, one of only twenty-four finishers out of the sixty cars which had started the car-killing enduro.

During the summer a special called the SR–2 was developed by Duntov for racers Jerry Earl, Dick Thompson and Curtis Turner. It was a Sebring-based car with an extended nose and a stabilizing rear fin. In 1958, this car was taken over by Jim Jeffords, who painted it purple and won the SCCA B-Production championship, dubbing his mount the 'Purple People Eater'. A red SR–2 built for stylist Bill Mitchell was more of a show car but it did finish a respectable sixteenth at Sebring in 1957, with Pete Lovely driving.

For model year 1957, important developments came thick and fast. The car itself was unchanged, but a four-speed gearbox was provided by mid-model year, the engine was enlarged to 283 cubic inches (4.6 liters), and a series of engine tweaks saw Corvette horsepower soar to 283 — the magic goal of 1bhp per cubic inch — thanks to all-new Ramjet Fuel Injection.

The engine mods began with a perfectly conventional, 0.13-inch overbore which, with the standard four-barrel carburetor, produced 220bhp at 4800rpm. The engine also featured longer-reach spark plugs, carburetor fuel filters, larger ports, wider bearings and oil-control piston rings. The optional dual four-barrel set-up gave 245bhp, and 270bhp with high compression heads. The now-legendary 'Fuelie' was the ultimate street package, offered in two stages of tune: 250bhp with hydraulic lifters, 283bhp with solid lifters and the Duntov cam. There was yet a further development for racers, the EN engine, adding cold-air induction system and identified by a special, column-mounted rev counter. Heavy-duty brakes and a tuned suspension were also part of the EN package. Officially the EN also developed 283bhp although some sources say it broke the 300 mark; even the 'street' engine was closer to 290bhp, and was later so listed.

Duntov sold fuel injection on its relative practicality compared with that other 'instant-power' modification popular at the time, supercharging. While the Studebaker Golden Hawk and 1957 Ford Thunderbird used superchargers to good effect, Duntov argued that they were an inelegant solution to the problem, generating high temperatures and dangerous internal stress when applied to typical production V8s. Duntov was, of course, European in his attitudes and prejudices: fuel injection was being tried with good effect by reputable European companies, so why not GM?

Although it was developed by Rochester Carburetor, the 'fuelie' was strictly a GM design. Its components included a special manifold, a fuel meter and an air meter, the latter directing the air to the intake ports, where a precise amount of fuel was injected to form the mixture. Petrol was delivered by a high-pressure pump driven off the distributor. The manifold was a two-part aluminum affair, the upper casting contained air passages and the meter system, and the lower casting contained ram tubes and a cover for the top of the engine. Dual exhausts were connected by a crossover pipe which equalized the exhaust flow through each muffler and prevented uneven distribution, retarding corrosion.

Unfortunately, the fuel-injection episode was not one of Zora's finest hours. Racing cars were often forced to eliminate the fuel cut-off to escape a flat spot when accelerating hard and the injector nozzles absorbed heat and caused rough idling, or suffered from dirt deposits. Street users found the injection system hard to service because it was unfamiliar to the average Chevrolet service department. Finally, the availability of a 270bhp engine using the more familiar carburetors made customers wary of spending the extra money for injection. Of the 6338 Corvettes in model year 1957, only 240 were injected; the system was also offered on full-size Chevy passenger cars, but these were even rarer. Fuel injection remained an option until 1965, and was improved considerably along the way, but it never caught on with customers. Because of that scarcity, 'fuelies' are today the most desirable Corvettes of the 1956–62 generation.

In the story of Corvette's coming-of-age as a true sports car in 1957, the four-speed gearbox cannot be forgotten. Like the injection system, it was built by an outside firm (Borg-Warner but designed to Chevrolet spec. Its genesis was the Borg-Warner three-speed previously used, with reverse gear moved into the tail-shaft housing to make room for a fourth forward speed. A $188 option introduced in May, it featured close ratios (2.20, 1.66, 1.31 and 1.00 to 1) and, hooked to a high-output engine and 4.11:1 rear axle ratio, produced astounding acceleration. A 270bhp Corvette with such equipment would deliver 0–60 in 6 seconds and scale the standing quarter-mile in less than 15 seconds doing 95mph. 'Fuelies', incidentally, were a shade quicker. . . .

Another sports-racing project, the Sebring SS, got under way in mid-1956. His eyes fixed on the Florida enduro (and if that brought success, Le Mans), Duntov started with a clean slate, tubular spaceframe chassis and de Dion axle, added a fuel-injected Corvette V8 engine and a lightweight magnesium body. On paper, the Sebring SS looked impressive, but at Sebring 1957 it failed to finish, although Dick Thompson/Gaston Andrey took twelfth place and first in the GT class with a production car. Before Duntov could rework the SS for Le Mans, Harlow Curtice announced the infamous Auto Manufacturers Association 'ban' on racing.

This curious decision, born of ignorant claims by the insurance industry and the growing safety lobby that factory racing encouraged dangerous driving, did not technically ban the manufacturers from carrying on as they had; it was simply an informal agreement 'not to encourage' references to competition in advertising, nor to provide racing teams with factory aid. It was adhered to, for a time, only because it suited the manufacturers. Car sales were at record levels and a truce between GM, Ford and Chrysler seemed perfectly agreeable, while American Motors and Studebaker-Packard weren't racing anyway so were happy to go along. Later, when sales were harder to come by, the big companies broke the agreement, first secretly then overtly. By 1965, most everybody had forgotten about it.

Although the AMA decision temporarily thwarted Duntov, it had no effect on the privateers. In late '50s America, Corvettes virtually owned big-bore production racing. Jim Rathmann and Dick Doane won the GT class at Sebring 1958 and Jeffords came back again in 1959 to win the SCCA B-production title with a production Corvette. At Pikes Peak in 1958, veteran hill-climb maestro Ak Miller drove a Corvette up the 14 000-foot mountain in 15 minutes and 24 seconds, beating everything else entered in the sports-car class. In 1960, Chuck Hall and Bill Fritts brilliantly won the Sebring GT title, while Briggs Cunningham's team of three Corvettes went to Le Mans, where Bob Grossman finished eighth — the highest Corvette score yet in international competition. The SCCA B-production title went to Thompson in 1961 and Don Yenko in 1962 — by which time full-race Corvettes were as common on US road courses as MGs and Triumphs.

After all the glories of 1956 and 1957, the story of the Corvette in the years leading up to the classic Sting Ray seems dull. But had it not been for the recession of 1958, we might have seen Corvettes that put everything else in the shade. What about an aluminum grand touring coupe with gullwing doors? Or a 1962 Corvette with four-wheel independent suspension, a rear-mounted transaxle with integral inboard brakes, dry-sump lubrication, an aerodynamic body in which windshield and side windows were all of a piece, and a curb weight of 2500lb? These thoughts and others like them occupied the more advanced Corvette thinkers in those years, although they did not become public knowledge until much later.

When such advanced concepts were first discussed it was 1956; Corvette fever was reaching peak proportions with the advent of the new generation and Corvette's simultaneous emergence as a competition sports car. The Corvette was hitting its stride, so it made sense to dream about future generations.

The gullwing was Harley Earl's idea: certainly, the smoothly rounded, flowing lines of the 300SL appealed to him, and certain contours of the production Corvette look almost too close to the SL for comfort. Unlike the Mercedes, this proposal contemplated conventional doors, with panels that flipped up from a centre axis through the fastback roof — automatically when a door was opened. Replacing fiberglass with some other body material was considered when engineers suggested going to a unit body/chassis, and this would have provided the aluminum body with the needed rigidity. Sweeping, pontoon fenders, which Earl had liked since the 1940s, were combined with quad headlamps, which were themselves just coming into vogue in Detroit.

At that time, the fiberglass body appeared to be the limiting factor in Corvette volume. 'We thought it was possible to produce fiberglass for just 10 000 cars,' Duntov said. GM body engineers — and the necessity of finding a way to expand production without chucking the material — eventually solved this dilemma, so the conservatives prevailed and the Corvette was merely facelifted for 1958. The general downturn in car sales, which followed that year, put a final end to Earl's visions of this radical coupe.

More radical yet was the Q-Corvette, conceived by Bill Mitchell after he had relieved Harley Earl as Chief of Design in 1958. Unlike Earl, Mitchell was attuned to the engineering side of the business, and worked closely both with racers like Dick Thompson and technical wizards such as Duntov. The Q-car was part of a radical revision across the boards at GM, evolving a full line of cars with rear-mounted transaxles and fully independent suspensions. The inspiration for this idea, of course, was Ed Cole's Corvair, the rear-engined compact then nearing release for 1960. The concept intrigued Corvette stylists, and numerous renderings of a Q-Corvette came off their drawing boards. But uncertainty about the Corvair's reception, plus concurrent industry sales problems, caused GM first to hesitate and then to write off the project. In a way, it was like the modern Saturn project — the scheme for a revolution in GM design on a division-wide basis which has been on and off again even more than the Q-car 30 years ago.

The 1958 Corvette thus emerged as just a facelift, inheriting some of the worst aspects of that model year at General Motors, heavy-handed styling, too much use of brightwork, greater length and bulk. Although it still retained the 102-inch wheelbase, the '58 proved about 200lb heavier and nearly 10 inches longer than the '57 Corvette, as well as 2 inches wider. The front end was very glitzy with its four headlamps, each pair trailing bright metal moldings down the tops of the front fenders. The grille teeth, though fewer, were heavier, and accompanied by auxiliary openings on either side. While the fender-top dummy vents of 1956–7 were gone, another assortment of dummy louvres appeared on the hood, and pseudo-extractor vents appeared in the cove molding ahead of the doors. A further two chrome-plated blades rode down the trunk lid. Detroit haters who had vilified the earlier models continued to lampoon the '58.

Yet it was an improvement in certain respects. The cockpit was more functional, with all the instruments grouped in front of the driver; the speedometer was set back from a large 6000rpm rev counter rising bolt upright above the steering column. Extra rigidity was provided by a center console, reaching down from the dash, containing the heating/ventilation controls and 'Wonder Bar' radio. Pressing the bar made the radio seek the next clear frequency, and the sensitivity of the search could be controlled separately. There was a locking glovebox in the vertical wall between the seatbacks, safety reflectors in the trailing edges of the armrests, new upholstery material and a grab bar for the passenger.

Mechanically, there were few changes. All engines and horsepower ratings were as before save the base engine, which now went to 230bhp. The high-compression 'fuelie' with its Duntov cam still belted out 290bhp but only 1500 'fuelies' were built for '58 and 500 of those had the standard-cam 250bhp engine. Close to half the '58s had the base engine, the rest, dual four-barrel set-ups with 245 or 270bhp. Although GM were officially out of racing, they offered a wide variety of performance options for the more competitive Corvettes, including the Positraction limited-slip differential, sintered-metallic brake linings (only $27 extra and worth every cent), heavy-duty springs/brakes/shocks. All these plus the 290 engine could be ordered for less than $5000 — roughly the same price as the Jaguar XK150S, which was Corvette's main sales competitor now that the Thunderbird had become a four-seat luxury car.

The racing success which continued to attend Corvette in 1958 was unmentionable at GM. Instead, we were treated to a lot of guff. The Corvette, adverts claimed, was 'beautifully compact', designed to 'cling to the road like a stalking panther', its 'silken cyclone of a V8' exploding off the line 'as easy as a giant's stride', with steering 'as sharp and precise as a scalpel'. 'Uncle' Tom

McCahill, *Mechanix Illustrated*'s king of the mixed metaphor, likened its performance to 'a tomahawk cleaving a soft scalp'. But that was America, those were the '50s, and there were still buyers aplenty for the Corvette, sales of 9168 rather making it the country's favorite two-seater.

One well known advantage of fiberglass was that it allowed rapid styling changes so in the Corvette's case, the normal 3-year lead-time between a styling idea and its appearance in production was unnecessary. Bill Mitchell replaced Harley Earl at styling in 1958, and set about instant corrections to what he considered an overdecorated Corvette. Off came the hood louvres and chrome trunk lid moldings and more thought was applied to the already much improved interior. Sun visors were provided for the first time; armrests were repositioned to better suit the 98th-percentile human, a T-shaped lockout was added to the gearbox lever to avoid accidental engagement of reverse, and seats were reshaped to hold the passengers more securely. The array of Corvette drivetrains remained the same, but an important change occurred in the suspension. Trailing arms were placed between the frame and rear axle to prevent axle wind-up under hard acceleration.

That the Corvette was ever subject to its status as a minor product of a very major corporation could be the theme of this book. GM's attitude was sometimes contradictory; its resources were virtually bottomless yet the Corvette had always to justify itself in the corporation's profit-oriented world. By 1959, the Vette had reached another turning point in its variegated history. Racing had become a dirty word, so did the Corvette still serve any purpose? Managers used to charting sales rather than lap times pointed to Ford's enviable success with the Thunderbird: since going to four seats and a larger, more luxurious design, T-bird sales had soared from nearly 40 000 in 1958 to 67 000 in 1959 and over 90 000 in 1960.

People like Bill Mitchell argued that the 'personal luxury' car as defined by the Thunderbird could be duplicated with a new product rather than an altered Corvette. In fact, that's what happened in the shape of the tremendously successful Buick Riviera, introduced in 1963. In the end, Mitchell said, the Corvette project was left alone: 'It was my pet. No high power in Chevrolet was interested — the volume and profit wasn't there. You could do what you wanted without anybody monkeying around. In the other divisions, when you'd have a showing, you'd have the chief engineer and six assistants plus an audience in the studio that would drive you nuts. Committees, committees, committees. The first Camaro and Firebird were so "committeed" that I don't remember what they look like. They were just nothing. The other ones we got done so damn fast that they never saw 'em! But with the Corvette, they would always leave you alone.'

They didn't give Corvette much money, however: the 1960 car was ordained to be another repeat of the 1958–9 formula. Engine modifications improved performance; an 11:1 compression gave the 'stage 2' injection V8 315bhp; 'stage 1,' with hydraulic lifters, produced 275. These gains precluded the Powerglide automatic option on 'fuelies'. Normally aspirated V8s were re-runs of 1959, incidentally. Duntov's influence saw increased use of aluminum in such components as clutch housings and radiators, a thermostatically controlled radiator fan and 24-gallon fuel tank, both of which were options.

The heavy-duty suspension option was dropped but a set of sway bars front and rear was now standard. Sales stuck around the 10 000 mark. Mitchell[1] was granted more latitude to alter the 1961–2 models, however, and these proved to be the nicest-looking Vettes since the '57.

[1] A note about spelling. Mitchell called his racing car Stingray, but the production Corvette bearing that name was called Sting Ray from its 1963 introduction through 1967. The new 1968 Corvette bore no special designation, but in 1969 the name was brought back as Stingray.

WILLIAM L. MITCHELL

A publisher friend of this writer happened to be in the toy department of a New York department store in the early '70s, overhearing a demand by a spoiled kid: 'I don't care, Mom, I've gotta have that remote-control Corvette model'. Mom let him have it. The only strange thing about this encounter was that the kid was pushing 60 and was Bill Mitchell, Vice-President for Design of General Motors.

'Big kid' is the kindest thing his critics say about him. The author has never forgotten the words of journalist Leonard Setright, laughing at Mitchell's 'round body, clad in mylar, astride one of his adolescent fantasy motor cycles. . .enough to force a guffaw from Samuel Beckett'.

Those who saw only the outlandish public face Mitchell chose to display to the world missed the fact that he was supremely competent — able simultaneously to judge both the public taste and exactly how far he could go in appeasing it. True, the public taste often demands vulgarity, and Mitchell dished it out at times during his 42 years of GM. He compared the traditional annual facelift of the '50s to bricklaying: 'You just laid the chrome on with a trowel'.

But the realist will look at Mitchell's long line of simply superb designs and conclude that, left alone, he was hard to beat. The 1961–2 Corvette facelift (conceived, crafted and wrapped up in a quarter of the time it normally required); the unimpeachable 1963 Sting Ray; the 1963 and 1966 Buick Rivieras; the elegant 1965 Corvair; the first Oldsmobile Toronado and front-drive Cadillac Eldorado; the 1970 Camaro; the 1975 Cadillac Seville — all these and countless other great designs made it through the leveling process of management review, production engineering, sales and accounting input, clay models, steel models, running prototypes and pre-production models almost intact.

Over many years, Mitchell's contributions to the Corvette were notable and influential. The Sebring SS, the SR–2, the XP–700, the skein of Mako Sharks with their shark-like paint jobs, the Mulsanne and the Sting Ray, the Astro II and Manta Ray (and above all the exciting Aerovette) collectively form the most free-wheeling and imaginative group of showcars and experimentals any manufacturer has produced in any country. Many of these, and the production Corvettes, too, *were* the work of talented underlings; but it was Bill who recognized their talent, and gave them an atmosphere that brought out their best.

The words of Jerry Palmer, chief stylist of the current generation Corvette, are the best tribute Bill Mitchell could have. Even though not everything about it pleases him, Palmer says, 'If Bill were running the studio, I don't think it would be a lot different from how it is today'. That's quite a compliment.

Genesis of the '61 facelift was Bill Mitchell's Stingray[1] Special, which he built on a rescued chassis of Zora Duntov's SS racer for SCCA class C-modified competition in 1959–60 (with Dick Thompson driving, the Stingray won the title in 1960 with three times as many points as the next car up, ironically without ever winning a race: it simply placed higher than anything else!). GM pointedly distanced itself from the Sting Ray Special and told Mitchell it would have to be strictly a personal project. 'I had GM engineers and a lot of talent at GM helping me,' Mitchell admitted. 'It cost plenty, all out of my own pocket, [but] on my income tax I got away pretty good. I couldn't afford to build and race the Stingray today, but back then, it pleased me no end to go up against Cunningham and those boys with the faster cars, and take any of them.'

It also pleased Mitchell to evolve the unique tail-end styling of the Stingray racer and apply it to the production 1961 Corvette. The simple, flowing creaseline, with its unique 'ducktail' back end, also appeared on the XP-700 showcar. Quad tail-lamps were inset, flanking the license-plate recess, and thin chrome bumper-guards bracketed the license-plate frame. It was very clean and functional looking, heightened by Mitchell's return to conventional tail pipes (routed out under the body instead of poking through the bumpers).

The front end was also transformed by Mitchell's stylists, who were told to dump the chrome and go for function. Headlamp bezels were thus finished in the body colour, while the grille teeth were replaced by a fine meshwork. The formerly divided bumpers were now connected by a horizontal bar, bisecting the grille and tied to slim vertical bumperettes. The round Corvette bonnet badget was replaced with Chevy's crossed-flags emblem, while the flags' place on the lower front fenders was taken by a small, neat oblong badge. Mitchell had not wanted to duotone *any* cove moldings this year; the sales department over-ruled him, offering the treatment as a $16 option. Although more customers ordered it, GM

Styling prevailed on the 1962 model and the option was deleted. Most 1961 Corvettes were also equipped with a heater ($102 extra), and about 7000 or three-quarters of production had the $188-extra four-speed gearbox.

Duntov's aluminum radiator was now fitted to all Corvettes as standard, cutting weight and giving a ten per cent improvement in cooling; side-mounted expansion tanks were added as a running change during the model year. The engine line-up was unchanged, but the hydraulic-lifter stage 1 injection version was boosted to 275bhp. This was to be the last year for the now-venerable Chevy 283 in a Corvette.

Powerglide was not available with the injection or top-horsepower carburetor engine. Even when combined with the basic 230bhp V8, however, a Powerglide-equipped Corvette could scale zero to 60mph in 8 seconds. Injected four-speeds could improve on that figure by 2–3 seconds, depending on gearing; top speed ranged between 110 and 130mph. The competence of the cars was demonstrated at Sebring '61, where a near-stock Corvette finished eleventh overall in the gruelling Twelve Hours against a field of very sophisticated rivals. Prices continued to creep up along with the performance, and sales of the '61 held at just under 11 000.

On the 1962 Corvette, Mitchell's men blacked out the grille, scrubbed the duotone cove panel with its chrome outline, and substituted a rather neat gill-like trim for the former chrome flashes in the fender scoops. A ribbed anodized aluminum molding trimmed the rocker panels, and the (optional) whitewall tires, like all their ilk from 1962 on, had significantly slimmer bands of white. These changes further improved and updated the Corvette's looks — but the big difference was the new, 327-cubic-inch (5.4-liter) V8.

Bored and stroked from the old 283, the 327 was to become a classic Corvette powerplant, lasting until 1969. Base horse-power was now 250; the previous twin-four-barrel version had been replaced by a single, larger-throated, four-barrel, yielding 300 and 340bhp and topping the range, the Ramjet fuel injection gave 360bhp. All three of these high-performance engines had larger ports and a longer-duration camshaft, while solid lifters were fitted to the 340 and 360 engines. 'Fuelies' were capable of standing quarter-mile runs which, a few years before, would have been considered in the dragster class at 15 seconds and 100-plus mph. Those with taller gearing could break 140mph. At the same time, the Corvette remained highly civilized for a sports car, with options like automatic transmission and (for the first time) air conditioning. Dual-purpose? It was more like four or five purposes!

The Corvette's loyal public responded warmly to the 1962 package. Sales totaled 14 531 — a clear record, up 33 per cent from 1961, and vindication of the now-distant decision to retain a true sports car among the Chevrolet sedans. Proven on the track as well as the road, the 1962 was the finest Corvette so far and the finest example of the American sports car, a breed born in the days of Mercer and Stutz.

'A cloud no bigger than a man's hand,' but one which made the traditionally skittish Chevy sales managers worry, appeared in 1961. It was a smooth, low, bullet of a sports car, all new from the ground up and priced squarely in Corvette territory. It also bore one of the most respected names in the business. As its maker cleverly announced to the American market, in a plain advert bearing only the car and a dummy postage stamp, as if it had been freshly posted. 'This is the New Jaguar XK-E!'

The E-type, as it was known in its homeland, was a sophisticated challenge. Its sensuous lines at once demonstrated the inherent age of the Corvette body, despite all Mitchell had done to keep it up to date. Although powered by a straight-six rather than a V8, the E-type boasted one of the world's legendary engines, the famous double-overhead-camshaft 3.8 that had won Le Mans for Jaguar more than once. Selling for $5695, about $750 more than the typically equipped Corvette, it offered what seemed like space-age styling and engineering in those days. It had four-wheel independent suspension, compared to the Corvette's beam rear axle; disc brakes where the Corvette had drums; an advertised (if optimistic) 150mph off the showroom floor, compared to the typical Corvette's 135; *and* there was a swoopy grand touring coupe model for $200 extra. Remarkably, the XK-E weighed less than 2500lb, against the fiberglass Corvette's 3000lb. This writer remembers his first published contribution to a motor magazine: a letter to the editor, favorably comparing XK-E to Corvette, and asking of the latter, 'How much would it weigh if it were steel?'

It is commonplace, but too easy, to say that the Corvette's response to the Jaguar threat — and threat it was — came one year later, in 1963. But that merely demonstrates ignorance of how the American industry works. Conceiving, styling and engineering the 1963 Corvettes took at least three years and had begun as far back as 1958 when Bill Mitchell decided to go racing with Zora Duntov's SS chassis. Mitchell himself takes credit for conceiving the name of this all-new and spectacular 1963 Jaguar rival: the Corvette Sting Ray.

Best Vettes

1957
Injection Four-Speed Hardtop

The connoisseur is driven by many passions, not all of them rational. The second generation Corvette offers countless exciting choices. The original '56, with its clean-lined beauty, is one of them; collectors always like the first of anything. What about the '61 — the first Vette to show the styling hand of Bill Mitchell? Or the '62 model (with Mitchell's art honed to a fine edge), powered by the 327 V8, that ultimate development of the Corvette small-block? But no. If you must pick one car from the 1956–62 range, take the 1957 'fuelie' with a factory hardtop.

Its strengths, both as a collector's car and a soul-satisfying sports car, are obvious. This was the first fuel-injection model and the first with over one bhp per cubic inch. Its clean styling was unchanged from the 1956 original: sensuously rounded, bereft of all the old clichés and without too many new ones. Our choice would naturally have to come equipped with the fine Borg-Warner close-ratio four-speed gearbox. Throw in the factory hardtop in this best of all possible worlds, because it was easy to remove, and very snug when installed, with good visibility. Most important of all, the '57 'fuelie' can go like hell.

Just how quick it *is* varies with the driver, and depends to a large extent now on how much said driver values this admittedly pricey collector's item, one of only 240 cars equipped with Ramjet fuel injection. Pushed with abandon, and total confidence in the durability of thirty-year-old mechanicals, one ought to expect 0–60mph in 7.5 seconds and the standing quarter-mile in 15–16 seconds at over 90mph using a middling 3.7:1 final-drive ratio. Later fuelies with up to 395 horsepower were commensurately faster but the '57 is plenty for most souls.

Granted, it doesn't stop particularly well, although its notorious brake-fade characteristics would be more worrisome on twisty European roads than under most American conditions. A partial cure is the famous Cerametallic brake option, with a whopping 188 square inches of swept area (curiously, this was reduced after 1957, when the forward shoes were lined over only half their length). However, the metallics are not for everybody. Corvettes so equipped carried a disconcerting placard: THIS CAR IS NOT FOR STREET USE. Until warm, they're grabby and tend to slew the car when applied hard. Anyone who has experienced the truly prodigious fade of stock Corvette drums on the way down a fast slope might, however, forgive this side effect. . . .

The power steering is light but positive, and the handling is as good as any

Best Vettes

beam-back-axle car short of a contemporary Alfa Romeo. But one doesn't want to apply all 300lb ft of torque on tight curves; that caused a reaction well known to Corvette racing drivers, culminating in what Dennis May called 'final, ultimate and irrevocable oversteer'.

The 1957 Corvette is blessed with another characteristic not generally shared by Detroit cars of any era: outstanding quality of fit and finish. All in all, it seems hard to beat among the many interesting and rapid cars of the 'second generation'. It was manifestly a car of its time, with all that that implies both for and against, but this very vintage character is what makes it so desirable today.

Best Vettes

1957 CORVETTE 579 B SPECIFICATION

ENGINE

Type	Small-block V8 with cast-iron block and heads and five main bearings
Bore	3.875in
Stroke	3.0in
Displacement	283cu in
Compression ratio	10.5:1
Valve gear	Two in-line valves per cylinder operated by single block mounted camshaft in centre of vee, via pushrods and independent rockers
Fuel system	Rochester Ramjet continuous-flow fuel injection
Maximum power	283bhp at 6200rpm
Maximum torque	290lb ft at 4400rpm

TRANSMISSION

Type	Four-speed manual
Ratios	1st 2.20:1 2nd 1.66:1 3rd 1.31:1 4th 1.00:1
Rear axle ratio	3.70:1
Body/Chassis	Two seat fibreglass convertible body on box-section steel X frame

SUSPENSION

Front	Independent with double, unequal length wishbones, coil springs, telescopic and anti-roll bar shock absorbers
Rear	Live axle with longitudinal leaf springs, telescopic shock absorbers and anti-roll bar
Steering	Worm and ball
Brakes	Drums all round, 11in dia, 314 sq in swept area, sintered metallic linings
Wheels/tyres	15in steel wheels with 6.70 × 15 crossply tyres

1957 CORVETTE 579 B SPECIFICATION
continued

DIMENSIONS AND WEIGHT

Length	168.0in
Wheelbase	102.0in
Width	70.5in
Track	57.0in front
	59.0in rear
Height	51.9in
Weight	2850lb

PERFORMANCE

0–30mph	2.4secs
0–40mph	3.4secs
0–50mph	4.9secs
0–60mph	6.6secs
0–70mph	8.8secs
0–100mph	18.2

Standing quarter miles 14.2secs

Top speed 135mph

Fuel consumption 14mpg

PAGE 65 The side grille treatment along with the alloy rocker panels denotes the '62 model year.

ABOVE & FACING PAGE The 160mph speedo hints that there is something special under the hood . . . and there was, in the shape of the 327cu in V8, which was a bored and stroked version of the 283. In the fuel-injected form shown here it produced a massive 360bhp.

FOLLOWING TWO SPREADS The cleanest of all rear end treatments was another distinctive feature of the '62 models.

ABOVE Chevrolet's Public Relations' department picture gives slightly the wrong impression — back then the Corvette sold to a good number of blue-collar workers too.

LEFT Corvette interiors of the '58–62 generation remained surprisingly similar, and the dashboard layout was superior both to its predecessors and following models.

FOLLOWING SPREAD A '58 Corvette at dusk with the two-tone treatment typical of the period.

PAGES 76/77 No shortage of dials in the '58 models, along with almost perfect symmetry.

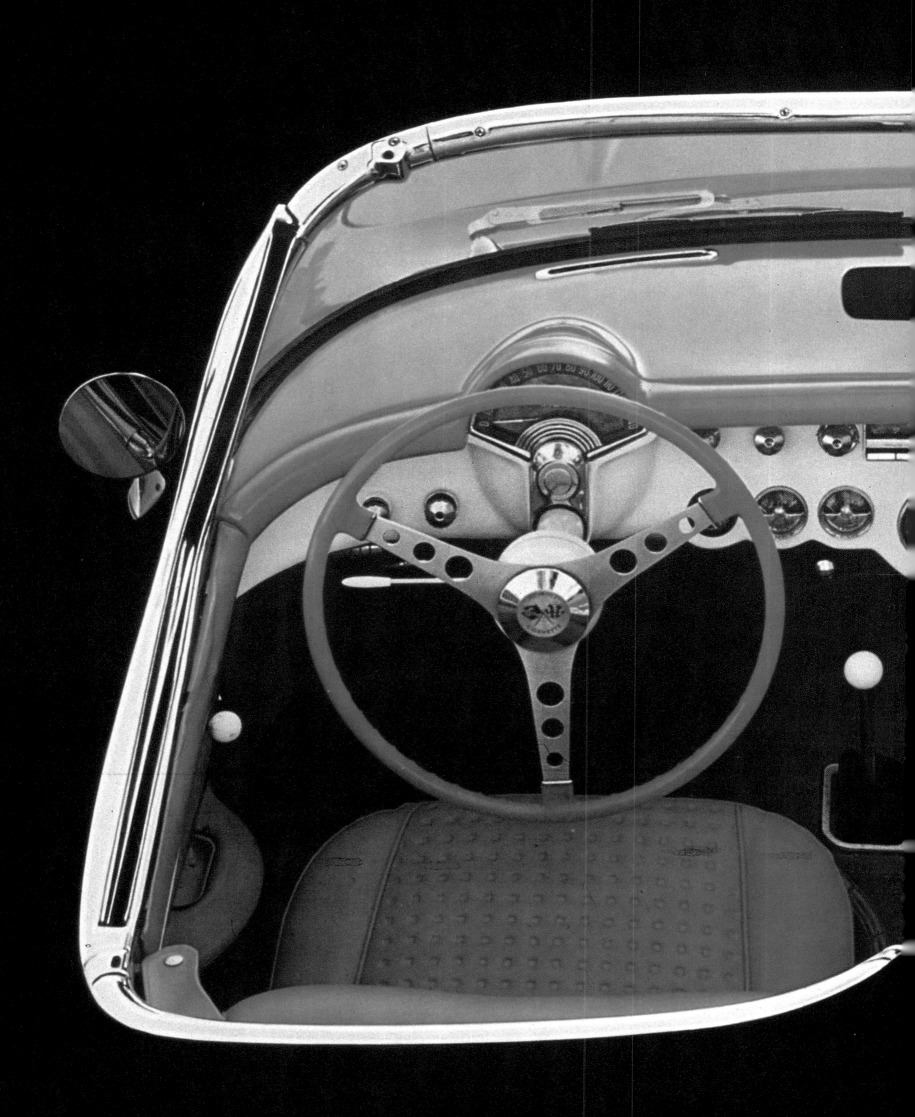

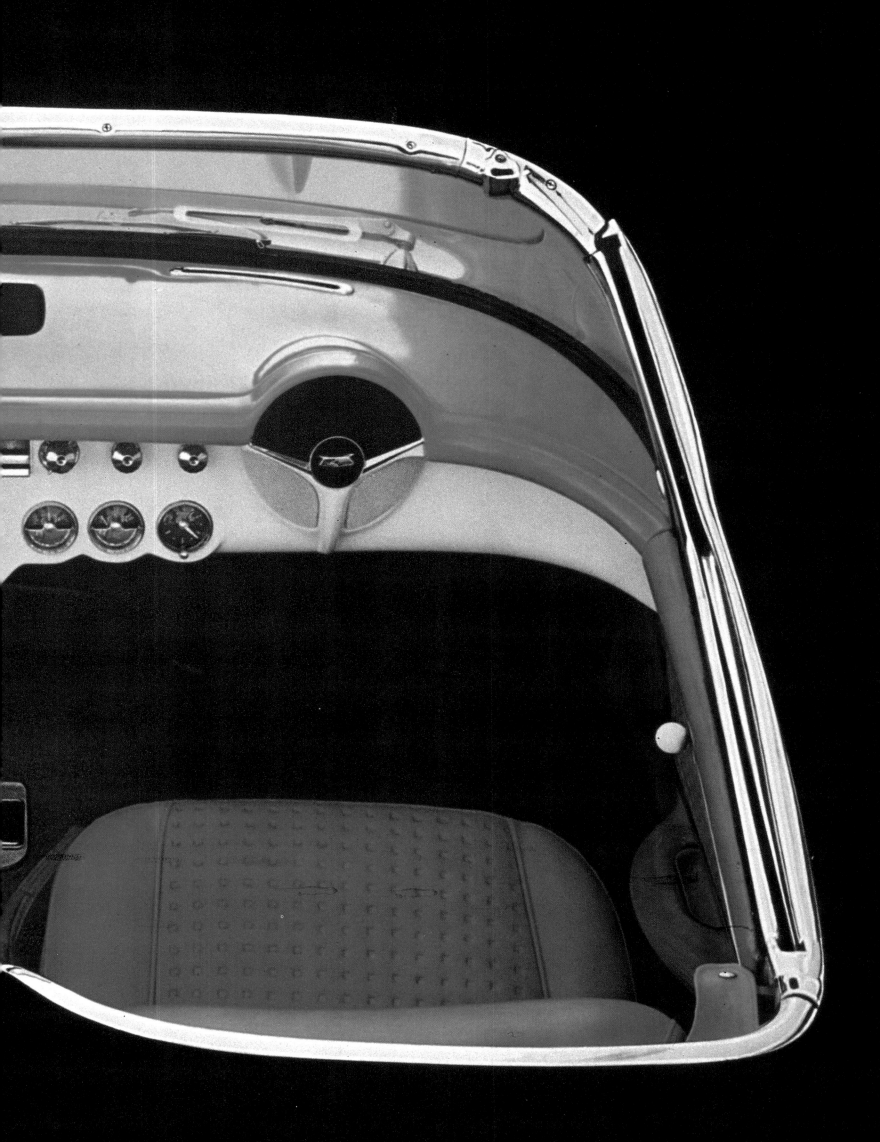

RIGHT Zora Arkus-Duntov at the wheel of the SS (Super Sport) Corvette, under the bubble canopy designed for endurance races. That canopy makes the car look less serious than it really was: under the bodywork was a tubular steel spaceframe, sophisticated de Dion rear suspension, a multitude of magnesium components for lightness, and enough power to have made the car a contender at the prestigious Le Mans 24 Hours in 1958 but for the AMA 'ban' on racing.

BELOW The Mako Shark of 1961 was aptly named, and although not a production car, contributed to the look of the '63 models.

BELOW RIGHT The far less exotically named XP-700 of 1958 sounds more like a roll of film than a Corvette. In three years design thinking had changed from this to the more successful Mako Shark shown opposite it.

ABOVE The shadowy outline shows that this is the frame of the '63–67 generation Sting Ray. Twin-wishbone suspension continued much as before, but the Sting Ray broke new ground in having independent rear suspension with a transverse leaf spring, a concept retained to this day.

RIGHT In 1963 coupe and convertible production was almost identical, with 10 594 coupes and 10 919 convertibles.

FOLLOWING SPREAD The '63 coupe was the only one of its generation to have the controversial split rear window.

TOP LEFT Chevrolet is a French name — the explanation for the tiny *fleur-de-lis* on the flag.

ABOVE Knock-off cast alloy wheels were a $322.80 option in 1963.

FAR LEFT & LEFT Important details of the '63 coupe: the Sting Ray badge, and the power behind the machine.

FOLLOWING SPREAD Along with the external restyling came a revamped interior, with the rev counter prominent as the 160mph speedo.

FACING PAGE 89 That distinctive split rear screen.

THE
BIG BANG

1963–1967

THE Corvette Sting Ray arrived with a bang: sales of the 1963 model-year cars — a fast-back coupe, now, as well as a convertible — surpassed 20 000 for the first time in history, and were almost equally divided between the closed and open versions. Actually, Corvette might have sold up to 30 000, had the production capacity been in place. The St Louis factory ran double shifts (also for the first time in Corvette history) and still couldn't meet the demand. Corvette inventories, which had hovered around 40–50 days before and had even been over 100 days in the grim early years, averaged two weeks in 1963. The reason for the improvement was not hard to grasp: the Sting Ray was simply the best Corvette the world had ever seen. Indeed, a large number of people think it is *still* the best.

Why was it so good? First because it represented something fairly rare in the high-volume American-car business: a model where everything came together beautifully. Styling, engineering, product planning, the model mix and option list, all combined to provide a brilliant sports car. The public responded and, over its 5 years, the Sting Ray sold more than 110 000.

None of this was preordained when Chevrolet began considering the options for a new Corvette generation around 1958. There was the Q-car, previously mentioned — radical, with rear-mounted transaxle, and smaller than the present models; the 1959 prototype XP-720, a racing coupe with a distinctive split backlight; and a simple reskinning of the 1958–62 'four-eyed' generation of Corvettes. Actually, the last-mentioned option was exercised somewhat in 1961–2, when Mitchell revised the rear end along the lines of his Sting Ray racing car. Ultimately, it was decided drastically to alter the Corvette design while making evolutionary improvements to the chassis, although not going all-out along Q-car lines, and retaining the existing range of small-block V8s.

These were good decisions because the 327, which arrived for the first time on the 1962

Corvette, was an outstanding engine with great flexibility; the chassis could easily be improved with all-independent suspension and, eventually, front disc brakes. The real challenge was styling — but Mitchell and Co would take on a challenge like that anytime. As Chuck Jordon, a Mitchell protégé and later GM director of design himself, told this writer years after: 'Cars like the Corvette are the stylist's "dessert"; they have the right lines, the size and proportions that encourage us to do our best, to have fun.'

They certainly had fun with this one, as the result proved. Actually, the coupe was designed before the convertible. As Chevrolet had never before offered a closed-body Corvette 'it had to be right, from the beginning', Mitchell said. 'It was a lot easier to perfect the coupe and then chop the top and make a convertible than trying to do things the other way around.' Naturally, the convertible continued to be available with a lift-off hardtop.

One influence from the XP-720 was the split back window, a design that has come to be a treasured distinguishing hallmark of the 1963 Corvette (a one-piece backlight replaced it on later models). Mitchell thought the 'split' was absolutely essential, unifying the roofline with the central 'points' on the deck and hood. Here he ran into opposition from his friend Zora Duntov, who hated the split window like poison: 'You couldn't see out the damn thing', Duntov exclaimed.

Mitchell gave in and changed the '64 model, but always regretted it. 'If you take that off,' he said of the dividing bar, 'you might as well forget the whole thing'. Coupes from '63 are always referred to as split-window Vettes and, because most collectors agree with Mitchell, the cars are worth more than the 1964–7 coupes.

Duntov and the body engineers exerted uncommon influence on the Sting Ray design because Chevrolet management was unanimous for the first time in demanding a genuine, dual-purpose, race-and-ride sports car, and Duntov's wisdom was respected even by the wildest chrome-happy Chevy stylist. Duntov wanted 'better driver and passenger accommodation, better luggage space, better ride, better handling and higher performance'. Nothing difficult about that!

Stylewise, these parameters required Mitchell's team to provide more interior space and luggage accommodation. The spare tire was placed in a special sub-floor housing under the luggage compartment. Although the only access to the coupe's storage area was from behind the bucket seats it was roomy. The cockpit was more commodious, too. All this extra room was obtained despite a 2-inch-shorter wheelbase and a narrower rear track. And, thanks to steel reinforcement, the cockpit was stronger and safer than before. Cowl-top ventilation and a much improved fresh-air heater were added creature comforts on the new model.

Bill Mitchell has always said he was happy to have retired when he did, when flat, squared-off, shapes were dominating the industry; he is much happier with the current rounded aero shapes. 'I can't understand Giugiaro,' Mitchell tells interviewers. 'All his cars look like they're made out of cardboard. You want to fold tab A into slot B'.

The Sting Ray bore out Mitchell's life-long involvement with overtly aggressive, flowing shapes: clean front fenders jutted forward, then tapered back to a 'coke-bottle' fuselage before the rear fenders kicked up again. A straight line broke up the body sides at mid-height, running right around the car, front, sides and rear. The sales department still demanded quad headlamps; Mitchell didn't like them on a sports car so he hid them, behind clever pivoting sections which were flush with the front end when closed.

'I hated those damn four-eyed monsters,' Mitchell later said, 'and covered them up whenever I could. Another example was the Riviera'. That was a reference to Buick's handsome personal-luxury car which also arrived in 1963; its quad headlights were stacked vertically, but by 1965 Mitchell had hidden them behind retractable panels as well.

Hidden headlamps had probably first appeared on Gordon Buehrig's famous Cord 810 in 1936, but had not been seen on an American production car since the 1942 DeSoto, of all things. Curiously, a DeSoto (the '55) also prefigured another Sting Ray feature: the 'gullwing' dashboard, in which two huge bulges encapsulated driver and passenger, meeting in the middle. The Corvette carried this junction down in a console containing radio and heater controls, and then between the seats. GM designer Dave Holls told the writer: 'The dual-cockpit was widely criticized as childish and overdone at the time. But it was a very fresh approach to two-passenger styling, and I think it worked remarkably well'. Chevrolet had to do something dramatic to compete with the rival Jaguar XK-E's row of smart white-on-black gauges set into an engine-turned metal panel.

Some more interesting detailed design, not all of it functional, was evident on the outside. One idea harked back to the still-born 1948 Tucker and the production 1951 Kaiser: doors cut into the roof to ease passenger entry. Unfortunately, they combined with the curved side glass to expose a lot of the cockpit to the weather, and one became fairly wet getting in and out of a coupe in a downpour. Mitchell also built dummy extractor vents into the coupe's corner posts, and into the front fenders of both models; they were just meaningless and would have been better left undone. Hood louvers, which were functional on Bill's Sting Ray racer, were also dummies on the production car.

The roadster, as well as the coupe, was sent to Cal Tech for extensive aerodynamic testing, including wind-tunnel evaluation. 'Today we have our own wind tunnel,' Chuck Jordon said later, 'but in those days we were exploring new ground. I don't think any American production car of its time was so thoroughly looked at from the aero aspect'.

One aerodynamicist at the GM Tech Center told this writer he thought the Sting Ray roadster was 'probably more slippery than the coupe. It has to do with what we call "perceived aerodynamics". For instance, Ford's Thunderbird looks swoopier than the notchback Mercury Cougar, but in fact the Cougar has a better coefficient of drag. The Sting Rays were probably similar in their relationship. But overall they were mighty good for 1963.' The CD for a Sting Ray was of the order of 0.37 — not very wonderful 25 years later, but almost space-age stuff in 1963.

While Corvette made do with the 1962 array of V8s (which, after all, had been new that year), the Corvette chassis was considerably modified, especially at the rear. Fully independent, three-link rear suspension with double-jointed open driveshafts, control arms and trailing radius rods now took the place of the traditional beam axle. One peculiar aspect was the springing — a single transverse leaf, seemingly far less sophisticated than the rest of the package. This was required because the new body style left no room for coil springs, and nobody would consider longitudinal leaves with this suspension. Duntov saw to it that the differential was bolted to the rear cross-member, and insulated with rubber at the mounting points. The frame itself was a well reinforced box.

Weight distribution on the new Sting Ray was much improved from the previous 55/45 to 48/52, giving a slight bias to the rear. Ride and handling were significantly better, and axle tramp had been eliminated. New recirculating-ball steering gear combined with a dual arm, three-link ball-joint front suspension to provide fewer turns lock-to-lock than ever before. Brakes were still drums all round, but the front brakes were wider and self-adjusting. An alternator replaced the generator, positive crankcase ventilation was provided, there was a smaller flywheel and a new aluminum clutch housing.

Underscoring GM's re-awakened interest in competition was a long list of heavy-duty options: stiff springs and shocks, a stiffer anti-sway bar, sintered-metallic brake linings, Al-Fin aluminum brake drums, cast aluminum knock-off wheels, dual brake master cylinder and a long-range, 36.5-gallon, gas tank.

The car-buff magazines were uniform in their praise of the new Sting Ray. 'Chevrolet builds a really superb new sports car,' headlined *Sports Car Graphic*, implying that, after all, the earlier models weren't so superb. 'America's Only Sports Car Joins the Front Rank At Last' — *Car and Driver* clearly had the same view. Hyper-critical *Road & Track* contented itself with facts only ('smaller, lighter. . .all-independent suspension'). But at the end of their road test the editors admitted: 'As a purely sporting car, the new Corvette will know few peers on road or track. It has proved, in its "stone-age form" [pre—1963], the master of most production-line competitors; in its nice, shiny new concept it ought to be nearly unbeatable.' Not quite.

As things turned out, it wasn't from Jaguar's XK-E that the Corvette had trouble. The Jaguar never seemed to do well in SCCA and endurance racing. Despite being booted up to class A-Production with the 327 engine, Dick Thompson handily switched from 1962 Corvette to Sting Ray to win the 1963 Class A title. In Class B, Don Yenko triumphed with a pre-Sting Ray Corvette in

1963, and Frank Dominiani won in 1964 with a similar car. Neither did the XK-E prove a serious sales rival: the Corvette outsold it three or four to one in most years.

But nobody had counted on Carroll Shelby, who dumped a 289 Ford V8 into an AC Ace, called the result the Cobra and simply walked away from all competitors. 'It seems that in a ridiculously short time, the Corvette has been clouted from its position of absolute primacy in large-displacement production-category racing,' said *Road & Track*. That was in June, 1963; the Sting Ray had not been a year on the market.

Even on the street, the Corvette could not rival the limited-production Cobra, which was a semi-racing machine even in its most refined state: spare, spindly, light (2000lb versus Corvette's 3000), virtually without creature comforts and blindingly fast. The high-output Fairlane V8 of the Cobra delivered 271bhp, against 360 in the top Corvette 'fuelie' — but that meant 7.3lb/bhp for the Cobra and 8.3 for the Corvette. The more typical, 300bhp Corvette had a power to weight ratio of 'only' 10.0. 'The results are exactly what theoretical considerations predict,' continued *Road & Track*. 'The "showroom-stock" Cobra will cut a standing-start quarter-mile in 13.8 secs, with a terminal speed of 113mph, while a Corvette, in similar tune, is about a full second slower and will reach not quite 100mph at the quarter-mile mark. In top speed, too, the Cobra has the advantage. Its nominal frontal area of 16.6 square feet gives it quite an edge on the Corvette, which is [despite all that careful aero work!] pushing away at 19.3 square feet of air, and the touring version of the Cobra will exceed 150mph (urk!), about 10mph faster than the Corvette — even when the Corvette has the "big" engine. . . . The airflow over the Cobra is probably not as clean as that over the Sting Ray, but the Cobra's advantage in frontal area cannot be denied. To counter that advantage, the Sting Ray would have to be 14 per cent "cleaner" than the Cobra — and it isn't.'

The Sting Ray's modern, sophisticated suspension was miles better than the Cobra's, which dated back to AC's Tojeiro-designed Ace of 1952. But the Cobra compensated by being much lighter; also, although it was not renowned for the ease with which it applied all that power to the road, its primitive handling was predictable enough to allow a Cobra to be squirreled around a road course with fair abandon — certainly enough to beat the typical Corvette. Finally, the disc-braked Cobra stopped better than the Sting Ray in competition conditions, although, as *R&T* reminded us, 'disc brakes have not yet proven to be as trouble-free in day-in, day-out service as the better drum-type brakes, which the Corvette has'.

Zora Arkus-Duntov took a racer's view of the situation with typical aplomb and honesty: 'It was clear as day to me that the Cobra [would] beat the Corvette. It was very powerful and weighed less than 2000lb. Shelby had the configuration which was no damn good to sell to the people, except a very few. But it had to beat the Corvette on the tracks.' This the Cobra did, as they say, 'in spades'. The only way to stop it, *Road & Track* said with prescience, would be to build a special lightweight racing Corvette. In mid 1963, Duntov did just that. He called it Grand Sport.

The Grand Sport was conceived in the summer of 1962 as a lightweight racer built in just enough quantity (125 was the figure mooted) to be classed as a production car, to lick the Cobras, which were already startling the racing world before the Sting Ray was formally announced. In the event, only five Grand Sports were built, all during 1963 — wild cars with hand-fabricated, lightweight suspensions and four-speed transmissions, a ladder frame with 6-inch diameter frame rails, and an experimental 377-cubic-inch version

of the Chevy small-block V8. It had an aluminum block and two spark plugs per cylinder and, equipped with fuel injection, was said to develop 550bhp. The body was based on the production Sting Ray coupe, but smaller.

Duntov hoped to start the GS campaign with a win or at least a good showing at Le Mans, where he predicted speeds of 180mph down the Mulsanne Straight. But bureaucracy interfered; Chevrolet decided the Auto Manufacturers' Association 'ban' on racing was still in effect, and the program was cancelled before the cars left Detroit.

The five cars were then fitted with stock engines and sold to Grady Davis, Dick Doane, Jim Hall and John Mecom, all long-time Corvette racers, who hired Duntov to prep them for competition. It was really a 'works' effort, but the operation was now 'private' enough to let Duntov get away with it. Roger Penske and George Wintersteen had successful seasons with two roadsters (created by shearing the tops of coupes) but because of their limited 'production' they had to run in the C-modified class rather than C-production. Dick Thompson came out of retirement, meanwhile, to drive Grady Davis' GS to a fourth place finish in the C-modified championship.

Mecom did score a moral victory of sorts at the Nassau Speed Weeks in early 1964, when he entered three Grand Sports in the unlimited class, equipped with the special 377 engines. They were 10 seconds per lap faster than the best Cobras. The trio reappeared at Sebring, but none finished. Wintersteen and Penske continued to race Grand Sports through 1966, but by then the cars were outclassed.

The old AMA 'ban' was particularly excruciating in this instance, because the Grand Sports certainly had the potential to beat the Cobra on its own turf — proving that a semi-competition Corvette was at least the equal of a semi-competition

AC. Had Chevrolet built the 100 or 125 needed to qualify the Corvettes as production cars, the Corvette-Cobra battle would have been resolved. Alas, that didn't happen, and no development was done in 1966. By then, Duntov had turned to the L88 big-blocks to battle the big-block Cobras — another losing battle. It wasn't until the Cobra left the market in 1967 (because of impending government regulations) that the Corvette was able to come back in production racing. The Cobra's victory was decisive, but it was never a fair contest considering the contenders' vastly different production runs.

The last year in which coupe and convertible sales were approximately equal was 1963. After that, the soft-top out-sold the coupe until the end of the Sting Ray generation in 1967. Mitchell said this was because a discerning public couldn't stomach what had been done to his split rear window, but in fact, the convertible was simply the preferred body style among sports cars. The coupe had sold as well as it had in its first year because it was so stunningly beautiful. And it did continue to sell at between 8000 and 9000 units every year. Oddly enough, when the new, 'fourth-generation' Corvette arrived in 1968, coupe sales soared and eventually eclipsed those of the open model altogether. That was probably because by then the convertible had grown to be a much more 'enclosed' car.

The most obvious change on the 1964 model was the coupe's one-piece backlight, but many detail changes were made to clean up the package. Here Chevrolet responded to the criticism of sports-car people: the '63 Sting Ray was all right, they said, except for all the useless, non-functional gimmicks.

Accordingly, the two dummy air vents on the hood were scrubbed, although their indentions remained for the time being. Curiously, while the simulated extractor vents on the rear roof pillars were said to be functional, they actually only worked on the driver's side. Designers should have paid more attention here, because interior ventilation was not good in the coupe and pivoting ventwings had to be retained throughout the Sting Ray generation to help alleviate cabin stuffiness. The rocker-panel trim lost some of its heavy ribbing, and the areas between the ribs were painted black to de-emphasize them. Wheel covers were made simpler, but still not nearly as handsome as the beautiful cast-aluminum knock-off wheels, manufactured for Chevrolet by Kelsey Hayes and costing over $300 extra. Finally, the fuel-filler door was given concentric circles around its crossed-flags motif.

Inside the car, 1963's color-keyed steering wheel was replaced by one with a simulated walnut rim. The shift lever was revised, with a new boot and bushings to quiet the linkage, which had been profoundly noisy the previous year. The din was further muffled by considerably more insulation, combined with new body and transmission mounts. Gauge bezels on the dashboard were painted flat black to minimize reflections, which had been a problem. Leather upholstery and the other interior options remained as they had been but, although leather cost a mere $81 extra, only about 500 cars had it in 1964. Air conditioning ($425) had been specified by only 278 Corvette buyers in 1963, and even fewer in 1964.

On the mechanical side, Duntov was striving for better ride qualities: the '64 thus changed from constant-rate to variable-rate front coil springs which were wound more tightly at the top, to preserve the ride as mileage mounted and shocks wore. An interesting change was made to the transverse rear spring, whose leaves now varied in thickness: the idea was that small bumps would affect only the low-rate areas of the leaves, while larger bumps would affect the high-rate areas, producing a softer ride without sacrificing handling on smooth surfaces. Shocks were also revised, given a small bag of freon gas within the fluid reservoir which absorbed heat and prevented the fluid from cavitating when heated by shock motion under rough road conditions.

All Corvettes in 1964 still came with the 327 cu in V8, again in four versions, starting with the hydraulic-lifter 250 and 300bhp units. The solid lifter, carburetor engine was pushed up to 365bhp with a higher-lift, longer-duration camshaft and a Holley four-barrel carburetor. The injection engine now developed 375bhp but its price, $538, was enough to turn away more than a handful of buyers. Transmission options were similar, but the previous Borg-Warner T10 gearboxes were replaced by GM units built in Muncie, Indiana, a standardization move but a good one. Muncie gearboxes, with their aluminum cases, had stronger synchromesh and wider ratios for better durability and driveability. These wide ratios were reserved for the 250/300bhp 'touring' engines, and were perhaps not as wide as the description implies: 2.56, 1.91, 1.40, 1.00; the close-ratio gearbox for the more powerful engines had 2.20, 1.64, 1.28 and 1.00 cogs.

A costly option in 1964 was the J56 sintered metallic brake package. Priced at $630, this included not only the special, fade-resistant, sintered metallic linings but the oversize brakes which had previously been offered as the Z06 option. The J56 package was really designed for competition — 'the harder these brakes have to work,' remarked *Car Life*, 'the better they are'. As before, the factory did not recommend the set-up on street machines, and took pains to avoid it being ordered by the general public. Until the advent of disc brakes the next year, however, it was the only sensible fix to a problem for which Vettes were notorious.

Sales were up slightly in 1964, with convertibles leading coupes now by a healthy margin: 13 925 to 8304. This ratio continued in 1965, when the little-altered Corvette sold over 23 000, a model year record — but records were being set almost every year now. The Sting Ray was a winning package.

Only the aficionado would notice the detail changes on the 1965 Corvette: a completely smooth hood, egg-crate grillework instead of horizontal bars, triple vertical fender louvres and slight alterations to the interior. Under the skin, though, one might encounter two new options: four-wheel disc brakes at last, and a jumbo V8, the 396-cubic-inch (6.5-liter) Mark IV.

The discs were four-piston types with twin calipers and cooling fins for the rotors, working through dual master cylinders serving front and rear. Pads were in constant contact with the rotors, but created little drag, and were said to last well over 50 000 miles in normal use. Swept area went from 328 square inches with the old drums to 461, a notable improvement. Virtually fade-free, the new discs were appreciated: although the drums were available in 1965 as a $64.50 credit option, only 316 Corvettes were so equipped, and for 1966 discs were standard.

The Mark IV engine was a 396 because GM policy had restricted small and intermediate Chevrolets to a maximum of 400 cubic inches. On Corvettes, the 396 replaced the 365bhp small-block option. It had 11:1 compression, solid lifters and a four-barrel carburetor, developed 425bhp at 6400rpm and a staggering 415lb ft of torque at 4000rpm. Of course, that was 'Stage 2'. If altogether too much, you could have 'Stage 1', with a 10.25:1 compression ratio and only 390bhp. . . .

In 1966, the 400 limit was waived, and a bore increase produced the 427. According to the manuals, this yet-larger engine had no more horsepower, but in reality it probably developed about 450bhp, and besides, it had 50lb ft more torque. This big-engined Sting Ray, announced by a special, aggressive looking, hood bulge and optional side-mounted exhaust pipes, was a profound performer right off the showroom floor. Common sense demanded that all 427s came with stiff front springs and sway bar, a special rear sway bar, an extra-heavy-duty clutch, and an oversize fan and radiator. The Muncie close-ratio gearbox and Positraction limited-slip diff were standard, as well.

For the ultimate in off-the-mark funsies, you could order the 4.11:1 final drive ratio, which casually produced 0–60mph in 4.5 seconds and 0–100 in a fraction over 11 seconds. Even with this ratio, the Mark IV would still do 140mph. With a more conventional 3.36:1 final drive, *Car and Driver* reported 0–60 in 5.4 seconds and a 12.8-second quarter-mile at 112mph. 'It's the power more than the engine that overwhelms every other sensation,' said *Car and Driver*. 'There's power literally everywhere, great gobs of steam-locomotive, earth-moving torque.'

Duntov, still out Cobra-hunting, thought well of the big-block as a possible snake-charmer. In 1966, he conjured up the L88 option: 427 cubic inches, 560 horsepower, the most powerful Corvette engine ever available. It was all Duntov's, no expenses spared, with a specification Zora had long dreamt about: aluminum cylinder heads with 12.5:1 compression ratio, full-race camshaft and 850cfm Holley four-barrel carburetor mounted on a special aluminum manifold. With it came a special chassis equipped with the F-41 handling suspension, heavy-duty brakes and Positraction. Exactly 20 L88s were installed in Corvettes, and at least three still exist. Production was no higher because even these proved insufficient to change things on the road courses. The Cobra had a 427 version now, too, and in SCCA

class A-Production the Cobras still showed their heels to the Corvettes.

In endurance racing, the big-blocks did rather better. In 1966, Penske, Wintersteen, Dick Guildstrand and Ben Moore combined to race a Corvette home first in its GT class at the Daytona Continental; they were also twelfth overall in an impressive field which included Cobras. At Sebring, they won another class title and finished ninth overall, a feat repeated again in 1967 by Dave Morgan and Don Yenko. At Le Mans the same year, Bob Bondurant and Guildstrand led the highly competitive GT class for several hours, until their engine blew up.

By the late '60s, Chevrolet was again interested in racing and everybody had forgotten the AMA 'ban'. But with the Cobra still ascendant in SCCA, Chevy turned to Trans-Am racing with the Camaro Z28. It simply wasn't possible to compete with the built-to-race Cobra with a Corvette manufactured primarily as a street machine, its terrific performance notwithstanding. But at the end of 1967 the Cobra retired: Federal safety and emission controls were coming in, and at the Cobra's sales volume it wasn't practicable to try to meet them.

Close to 28 000 1966 Corvettes were sold, convertibles leading by almost two to one. Changes that year were very minor indeed. The coupe's rear roof pillars were shorn of their extractor vents, dummy and functional – the latter hadn't done the job and everyone agreed they just looked dumb. Side-mounted exhaust pipes could be had in the small-block cars as well as those equipped with the Mark IV engine. But one old-time piece of Corvette religion was missing: fuel injection had disappeared, discarded in favour of cubic inches, which still counted for more than anything else in Detroit.

The '66 looked good, better than ever, in fact, and the '67 topped it. Later, many would look upon this final version of the Sting Ray generation as the best of the series, perhaps the best of them all. 'It finally looks the way we thought it should have in the first place,' said *Road & Track*. 'All the funny business — the fake events, extraneous emblems and simulated-something-or-other wheel covers — is gone, and though some consider the basic shape overstyled, it looks more like a finished product now.'

Five small, unified, fender vents replaced the three verticals; flat black and aluminum rocker panels gave a slimmer side profile; a single reversing lamp was mounted above the license plate; slotted, 6-inch Rally wheels replaced the old-fashioned wheel covers and were supplied with chrome beauty rings and lug nuts concealed behind small chrome caps. But the Kelsey-Hayes cast-aluminum wheels were scrubbed from the option list.

Interior changes were modest, as usual: new upholstery patterns, a shift of the parking-brake lever from beneath the dash to between the seats where it belonged. The optional hardtop for the convertible was offered with black vinyl topping, but this '60s fad was not popular with Corvette folk. Engine choices were now little changed, with the small-blocks continuing as before and the Mark IV rated again at 390 horsepower in its mildest form. Above it were a pair of high-performance 427s with 400 and 435bhp. Both carried three twin-barrel carburetors; the difference was in compression ratios: 10.25:1 and 11:1, respectively.

It was generally known around Detroit that the 'third generation' Corvette was now on borrowed time; several reporters let on that the '67 might not have appeared, had its successor been ready in time. Chevrolet, now fully on board with the Corvette as both a profit-maker and a showroom traffic builder, had wanted to replace the Sting Ray with an all-new car in 1967. But the new shape, designed by Dave Holls, did not prove very good aerodynamically. During wind-tunnel testing, it actually showed itself *less* slippery than the Sting Ray! Zora Duntov, who was a force on a par with God in those days, prevailed upon GM to hold the new car back until the aero figure could be improved. Hold it they did. The old formula remained popular enough to move nearly 23 000 Sting Rays in its final year.

Looking back, Bill Mitchell ranks the Sting Ray as the Corvette's finest hour — at least in the years when he was around: 'I just took all those lines and turned the Stingray racer into the production 1963 Sting Ray'. This wasn't strictly correct, but what follows is: 'That made the Corvette. And overnight, the sales just boomed. So I knew I had something. I went to the races in Europe and saw the cars there. I didn't want a car that looked like everything out of Europe. All their cars looked like Ferraris or Maseratis. They didn't have any sharp identifying features. I wanted a car that, by God, you'd know a mile away. That was my whole theme. And it did have identity.'

It sure did. The Corvette Sting Ray of 1963–7 was a tremendous statement of American automotive art. Like all art, it didn't appeal to everybody; nor was it arguably the best that could be done on a sports-car platform. The XK-E was smoother, the Aston Martin more functional and the Cobra more effective.

Taken as a whole, though, it is hard to think of any other range of Corvettes as impressively beautiful, as fleet and as well liked today. Car for car, 1963–7 Sting Rays bring the highest bids at auction, have the highest potential for future appreciation, and are more admired among Corvette people than anything else in the Corvette lexicon. All the more amazing, they were products of the highest volume company in the world, whose success rested on the millions of family clunkers it turned out every year.

General Motors was a different company in those days, however, less homogeneous, more enthusiastic about what it was doing — and better able to countenance the existence of a few gifted individuals.

GM-bashing is all too easy. Hindsight is cheap, and — some might say — far too readily indulged, yet it seems that the GM of today could learn a lot from the way the company handled the Sting Ray, and those who designed and engineered it, allowing those talented people enough latitude to produce something extraordinary and worthwhile, its achievements a benefit to the corporation as a whole.

Best Vettes

1963
Sting Ray Coupe

In September 1983, *Life* magazine assembled a number of automotive experts, all of whom had good credentials, to select the ten best and ten worst American cars of all time. Whether by accident or design, however, the panel had an average age of 50-plus, and naturally tended to praise antique, veteran and vintage machinery while deprecating most of the cars built after the war. Only one post-war car was named in the 'ten best' list, while eight made the 'ten worst', including no fewer than seven from the 1957–9 model years. The only post-war 'best' car was the 1955 Chevrolet Bel Air V8 — a curious choice, since it was outshone by the 1957 Chevy. But never mind.

Most remarkable was that this panel of experts overlooked what was certainly one of the most beautiful, best performing American cars of all time: the 1963 Corvette Sting Ray coupe.

Ask anyone remotely knowledgeable about Corvettes which car he or she would prefer out of the Sting Ray generation, and chances are they'll name this one — unless they are determined to have what later ad copywriters termed '93 million-mile headroom'.

Obviously, this writer agrees completely with Bill Mitchell: 'the split rear window really *made* the Sting Ray coupe and, if you take it off (as Chevy did in 1964), 'you might as well forget the whole thing'. This is a car with a definite 'face' and 'tail', emphasized by the body lines coming to a point on the hood and deck; the split window ties the whole together perfectly. Granting all the objections to the original '63 Sting Ray — it *is* full of non-functional trim bits and simulated this-and-thats — I still believe the original split-window design is the best of the lot, including the finely detailed 1967 model, which was certainly the cleanest.

The ultimate Sting Ray would, of course, have to come with the handsome Kelsey-Hayes cast-aluminum knock-off wheels, which cost the 1963 buyer $328, and are worth over $1000 in today's money (likewise on today's Corvette market). But, since my stable of best Vettes already includes the 1957 'fuelie', I would specify the non-injection 300bhp engine — only one step up from standard and not at all highly stressed — with the slick, four-speed Borg-Warner T10 gearbox and, say, a 3.36:1 final-drive ratio.

These choices would get the most out of the Sting Ray's greatest mechanical

Best Vettes

innovation: its chassis. Past Corvettes had been limited in this department by the need to use off-the-shelf Chevrolet production-car components. While lots of 'factory' modifications were available for racing, roadability of 'street' Corvettes remained lacking by comparison with the best contemporary European sports cars. The new, fully-independent Sting Ray suspension altered this situation drastically. It was not yet perfected, of course, and on rough surfaces it can get fairly dicey; but on smooth roads, which are mainly what we have today, it could hardly be better.

The cornering stability of these Sting Rays under such conditions is excellent. Although there is some understeer, a flick of the wheel takes the car off the predetermined line with no problems. Tempting criticism, I would even specify the optional Saginaw power steering, which provides only three turns lock-to-lock and has enough road feel to avoid the lightness and insensitivity of earlier GM power units.

As for performance, a Sting Ray coupe equipped in just this way returns 0–60 in under 7 seconds, cruises at 110mph and has a top speed of 120. What more could one want? Air conditioning, perhaps. Only 278 Corvettes had it in 1963 — but since this is an exercise in theoreticals, why not?

Best Vettes

1963 STING RAY COUPE L84 SPECIFICATION

ENGINE

Type	Small-block V8 with cast-iron block and heads and five main bearings
Bore	4.0in
Stroke	3.25in
Displacement	327cu in
Compression ratio	11.25:1
Valve gear	Two in-line valves per cylinder operated by single single camshaft in centre of vee, via pushrods and rockers
Fuel system	Rochester Ramjet continuous-flow fuel injection
Maximum power	360bhp at 6000rpm
Maximum torque	352lb ft at 4000rpm

TRANSMISSION

Type	Four-speed manual
Ratios	1st 2.2:1 2nd 1.64:1 3rd 1.3:1 4th 1.0:1
Rear axle ratio	3.70:1

SUSPENSION

Front	Independent with double, unequal length wishbones, coil springs, telescopic shock absorbers and anti-roll bar
Rear	Independent with single transverse leaf spring, trailing radius arms, lateral lower arm with semi-axle acting as top suspension arm, telescopic shock absorbers and anti-roll bar
Steering	Recirculating ball
Brakes	Drums all round, 11in dia, sintered linings 334sq in swept area
Wheels/tyres	15in steel wheels with Firestone 7.60 × 15 crossply tyres

Best Vettes

1963 STING RAY COUPE L84 SPECIFICATION
continued

DIMENSIONS AND WEIGHT

Length	175.3in
Wheelbase	98.0in
Width	69.6in
Track	56.3in front
	57.0in rear
Height	49.8in
Weight	3150lb

PERFORMANCE

0–30mph	2.9secs
0–40mph	4.1secs
0–50mph	5.1secs
0–60mph	6.5secs
0–70mph	8.3secs
0–80mph	10.2secs
0–90mph	12.7secs
0–100mph	14.9secs

Standing quarter miles 14.6secs

Top speed 147mph

Fuel consumption 16mpg

ABOVE The split-screen model was also one of the very first cars in the world, let alone the USA, to have doors wrapping around into the roof line.

FOLLOWING SPREAD A '63 or '64 convertible? The black recesses to the instrument faces indicate that this is a '64, the first year that you could get transistorized ignition, demonstrating that the Corvette kept abreast of technological development – indeed, it was often to the fore, fuel injection being another good example.

PAGES 108–111 The last of the Sting Ray generation, the '67, is recognizable by its five fender slots.

The 427cu in engine was an option, the 327 being the standard powerplant. It came in various stages of tune – 390, 400, 430 or 435bhp – and the 435bhp L71 had the further option of alloy cylinder heads, an option only 16 customers took up.

FACING PAGE 113 The Mako Shark II show car appeared in 1965 and set the style of the '68 to '83 generation.

WEATHERING
THE
STORM

1968 – 1982

Until the 1970s at least, the Corvette always had the benefit of enthusiasts at the helm, deftly guiding it along lines of development which other enthusiasts, by and large, approved. Had Ed Cole not come along as Chevrolet general manager when he did, for example, the odds are that the Corvette would have been written off as a bad job after the first generation's dismal sales showing. When Cole moved up in the GM hierarchy in 1961, his place had been taken by Simon E. (Bunkie) Knudsen and he carried on Cole's work, supporting the efforts of Mitchell, Duntov and their respective teams in developing the Sting Ray.

Knudsen left Chevrolet in 1965 and was replaced by Elliott M. (Pete) Estes, later to become GM President. Although both Knudsen and Estes had come from Pontiac, the resemblance ended there. Estes, wrote Karl Ludvigsen, 'had solid engineering credentials after a duty tour with the GM Research Labs and a spell as Pontiac's chief engineer. More of a team player than Knudsen,

the tall, mustachioed Estes soon involved himself in all aspects of the vast Chevrolet organization.' Estes backed the Mark IV V8 to the hilt, turning aside objections by corporate bean counters and rulemakers that it ought not to be provided in a small car; its benefits to Chevrolet have already been outlined. Significantly, Estes found himself at Chevrolet just as the all-new fourth-generation Corvette was being planned: here he was delighted to play a leading role.

During those uninterrupted years of record-breaking volume throughout the industry, no one could foresee the perils of the 1970s. No one (with the possible exception of Ralph Nader) could imagine that Americans would ever seek a substitute for cubic inches. And certainly no one anticipated that the body chosen for the Corvette in 1968 would last — indeed would *have* to last — 15 years.

Had some of the more radical ideas prevailed, the car would not have been anything like as stale as it was by the end of its life in 1982. A leading contender among many proposals was a rear-engined configuration, promoted by both the Engineering Center R&D Group (under Frank Winchell) and Zora Arkus-Duntov's Corvette Engineering Group. The Winchell proposal involved a short-wheelbase coupe with a backbone chassis-frame and full independent suspension, powered by a 327 V8, weighing 2640lb with a radical 30/70 front/rear weight distribution. Duntov's group envisaged a more conventional platform type frame with a Mark IV engine mounted ahead of the back axle, clothed in a body based on Mitchell's Mako Shark II prototype. But Mitchell was already another jump ahead, developing new, swoopy, curvaceous designs using Endura-coated bumpers – a breathtaking design off the board of Larry Shinoda.

According to Ludvigsen, 'the overwhelming cost burden of the required transaxle was the main obstacle', standing in the way of either the Winchell or Duntov proposals, and the final decision was to continue with the same basic chassis as the Sting Ray. Time was also a factor: the new Corvette was slated to debut in 1967.

The emerging design, productionized by Henry Haga under the general direction of Chevrolet chief stylist Dave Holls, embodied elements of both the Mako Shark II and Shinoda's clean-slate proposal. At this point, the car was being developed strictly as a coupe (although a removable backlight and removable roof section above the seats were included in the package); a convertible would also be offered, but that could easily be engineered later. A Targa-style top, like that of the Porsche, was also considered a possibility.

The production prototype looked clean and aerodynamically efficient, but proved less so in practice: at 120mph, the front end lifted over two inches and even the rear came slightly unglued. A rear spoiler was added to hold the back down. . .but it pushed the front up close to three inches! Finally, a front spoiler brought that end down and also eliminated drag, which had actually been higher on the '67 prototype than on the production '65 Sting Ray. In the end, it took only 105bhp to move the '68 at 120mph, against 125bhp for the Sting Ray.

Duntov, however, did not like the shape. The low roof dictated a short backlight which, with the rear spoiler, limited visibility. The front fenders were too high and the driver's sense of where the front of the car ended was vague. There was also considerable doubt about the new body's cooling ability, especially with the Mark IV engine. Duntov took his complaints to Pete Estes who made the decision to delay the new car a year, filling the gap with another round of third-generation cars.

Serious wind-tunnel work ensued. The fenders were lowered, the original fastback roofline became a slight notchback, spoilers were reworked and backlight glass area increased while more minor design problems were also fixed. Although Duntov was briefly hospitalized in the spring of 1967, he was back on the job by mid-year and was later promoted to become Special Consultant to the head of Chevrolet Engineering. In this role he was involved in many projects besides the Corvette but the Vette remained his baby and he continued to influence its design.

The cooling problem was only partially alleviated by larger front fender louvers, which had the side benefit of decreasing wind resistance, but the fourth-generation cars' cooling remained only adequate (Mark IV owners should turn the air conditioning off in heavy traffic). Hidden headlamps and hidden wipers (behind a small pop-up valance), features of the Mako Shark II, were important aero aids; these operated flawlessly and fast, actuated by vacuum cylinders. Small monitor lights were mounted in the center console to warn if any exterior lights failed.

The all-new 1968 Corvette ('Sting Ray' was dropped that year) arrived on time in the fall of 1967 and received the expected enthusiastic press. Automatic transmission was the important new Turbo-Hydramatic, but otherwise there were no drivetrain changes from 1967. Still listed was the L88 racing powerplant, which gulped 103 octane gasoline to satisfy its 12.5:1 compression ratio.

The '68 was lower, longer and wider than the car it replaced. That was only accidental; many years had passed since that trend had been *de rigueur*. There was no change in wheelbase, which remained at 98 inches, and the slightly wider track was due to the standardization of 7-inch wheel rims for the new, low-profile tires. True to the stylists' hopes, the coupe ended up Targa-like: two roof panels and the rear window could be removed to create a near-convertible without sacrificing the tightness and quiet of a permanent top when necessary. There was, of course, a full convertible as well, with an optional hardtop. As time passed, however, the flexibility of the coupe made the convertible superfluous, and it disappeared altogether in 1976.

If the drivetrain was familiar, the suspension was different, at least in detail, with handling the goal. The rear-suspension inner pivots were relocated to lower the roll center dramatically from 7.5 to 5.0 inches. The front springs and anti-sway bar were beefed up, and shock-absorber capacity increased. Thus, explained road-tester Jerry Titus, 'while the front-to-rear roll couple has been altered, overall chassis roll remains about the same since the rear springs are effectively softer in roll due to the increased leverage of the weight mass there'. In practical terms, the inside rear wheel stayed firmly anchored to the ground on cornering, increasing maximum cornering power from .75g to .85g. The change also reduced understeer

without sacrificing stability, decreased squat under hard acceleration and nosedive under braking. Titus noted that, although his first test car was a Hydramatic-equipped 427 which probably weighed 100lb more up front than a 327 stickshift, 'its understeer was light enough for throttle-induced oversteer to be easily attained and balanced'.

Of course the wider tires had a great deal to do with the better handling. Radials were still in the Corvette's future and with bias plys it was important to lay down as wide a paw-print as possible. Nylon tubeless F70x15s did just that, providing more consistent cornering characteristics: 'When cornering less than flat-out in the old car', one tester noted, 'cranking on a certain amount of lock to maintain a given line was impossible, and constant, nagging, corrections had to be made. Things improved as you cornered harder and took up some of the slack in the system, but the earlier action was far from confidence inspiring. On the other hand, the new car has far less difference in feel between medium and flat-out and consequently takes less getting used to.'

True, Corvette power steering was still a mixed blessing: it decreased the number of turns lock-to-lock, but tended to over-correct after an initial lag. This was noted by Titus and many others. In the car's defence Duntov said that 'slight adjustments to either caster settings or the spring rate in the power steering relief valve would probably correct it'.

These seemingly minor changes were significant. Corvettes for years had a reputation for unsophisticated handling, and that's being charitable. Watching Bob Grossman or Dick Thompson squirrel one of them around a tight road course like Lime Rock, Connecticut, this writer was firmly convinced that it took a brave man to master one, especially in the wet.

The fourth generation changed all that; it was the best handling Corvette yet. Summarized Jerry Titus: 'The Corvette is a very sophisticated, high-performance car with a fully adjustable and partially "tuneable" suspension. A buyer may luck into one with all its settings at the "right" end of the tolerances to utilize its maximum potential, but he's going to have to be a highly skilled driver and car-sorter to even know if it's there or not.'

Shifting to cosmetics, the '68 was clearly a state-of-the-art design. It lacked the classic drama of the Sting Ray, but the low hoodline, prominent fenders and carefully located air dams all bespoke a concern for aerodynamics that had not existed when the Sting Ray was born. Federal safety mandates caused the '68 to feature several new items: flush hardware, extra-thick dashboard padding, a rear-view mirror designed to break away if struck with serious force, marker lights front and rear. Another feature was the exterior door buttons, recessed into the door and covered by a spring-loaded metal panel. You reached into the hole, and pressed the button with your thumb — neat and aerodynamic.

The cockpit was little changed, although the minor gauges and some other controls had moved into a wider center console, where they were harder to see at a glance. The seats were redesigned and raked back 33 degrees (more than before) to provide decent headroom. Vent windows, which had featured on every Sting Ray, were eliminated in favor of 'Astro' flow-through ventilation. This was no substitute for the optional air conditioning but at over 50mph it did force a decent blast of fresh air into the car. Some 5000 people ordered air conditioning on the 1968 Corvette, but not for that reason — 'factory air' was simply becoming a popular option on all American cars.

Getting the car into production on time caused certain corners to be cut, and the quality of fit and finish on the 1968 model was probably the worst since the primitively hand-built 1953 models. *Car and Driver* actually called their sample 'unfit to road test', and said (in language much too polite for that magazine today) it had 'a shocking lack of quality control. . . . Few of the body panels butted against each other in the alignment that was intended. Sometimes the pieces chafed against each other, sometimes they left wide gaps, sometimes they were just plain crooked. . . . With less than 2000 miles on it, the Corvette was falling apart.'

Construction quality improved markedly in 1969 and 1970, but the initial bad press didn't help the new model. More fundamental was the very nature of the new Corvette. It seemed, as *Road & Track* put it, to have moved 'away from Sports Car and toward Image and Gadget Car'. They liked the driver/steering-wheel relationship, but hated the contortions necessary to get in and out, and the more distant positioning of the minor gauges.

Another problem not mentioned at the time was to be voiced more often as the years wore on — the 'bathtub' feeling of the new body. The '68 lacked the commanding driving position of its immediate predecessor and shorter drivers felt almost swallowed up by it. This reputation never really left it, and neither did the impression of noise and loose assembly: Paul Frère, given a specially prepared Mark IV coupe to try by his friend Duntov, declared the body 'noisy and full of rattles'.

There is another side to this coin; the Corvette went like almighty clappers, especially when equipped with the Mark IV engines. 'Maybe it's noisy, rough and uncivilized,' wrote *Car Life*, 'but you'd better believe that it takes a lot of car to catch this bear'. As Paul Frère admitted (in *Motor*) after only a few laps of the Zolder circuit in Belgium, 'I was lapping in the 1:57 bracket, much faster than I had ever lapped in a road car. As a basis for comparison, some other best times have been 2:07.5 with a Mercedes 250SL, 2:05.2 with a Porsche 911 (a 911S would probably take one second less) and 2:04.0 with a Mustang Hi-Performance, with handling kit. Even my best lap of 1:57.0 could probably have been improved by a second if the track had been completely dry.'

Criticisms aside, the new Corvette sold very well, indeed. For the '68 model year, the totals were 18 630 convertibles and 9936 coupes (the last year the former would outsell the latter). This was a new model-year record, just outscoring the previous best year, 1966. But with people like Estes and Duntov listening to the criticisms, the Corvette was bound to get better fast. The 1969 was improved in many ways, readopted the famous name Stingray (one word, now), and topped all previous records with a sale of nearly 40 000 units.

Major changes first: the wheels, which had been slightly wider in 1968, were now significantly wider at 8 inches, making them the widest in the industry. Alas, a side benefit was a very stiff ride, which all Corvettes of the fourth generation suffered. Frame stiffening (notably diagonal braces between the middle cross member and side rails) eliminated much of the shudder that had accompanied the '68. Detail changes were made to the interior to provide more room for the occupants.

The engine line-up was altered from its 1967–8 array, Chevrolet offering no fewer than *five* 427 engines. Three were street versions, packing 400, 430 and 435 horsepower. The L88 racing engine, which had been around for two years, was again available for competition; it was accompanied by a new ZL-1 version with dry sump and aluminum block, which was another $3000. Both L88 and ZL-1 had 'open-chamber' cylinder heads — with combustion chambers opened up on the side facing the exhaust ports.

'The power output *was* better with the new chamber,' wrote Karl Ludvigsen, 'not because it breathed better but because it had less surface area through which heat could escape to the coolant. But its reduced "quench" area [where the piston and head approach each other closely at top dead center] made it more prone to detonation that could destroy pistons, and demanded that the clearance between piston and head be set and maintained as close as possible. Ironically, this was easier to do with the iron L88 block than with the ZL-1, whose aluminum block tended to expand more as it became hotter. For sheer power, the L88 was the choice, while for power from a light engine and car the nod went to the ZL-1.'

The ZL-1, assembled using carefully balanced parts with the L88 at Chevrolet's Tonawanda, New York, engine plant, was said to produce 585bhp (gross) at 6600rpm — yet a Corvette so fitted weighed under 3000lb. As a drag racer it was almost unbelievable, achieving times that amaze and astound anyone used to today's fastest production machinery. A typical quarter mile performance was 125mph over an elapsed time of 11 seconds. Gorilla-tactics would actually improve on that. Wrote Eric Dahlquist: 'The ZL-1 doesn't just accelerate, because the word "accelerate" is inadequate for this car. It tears its way through the air and across the black pavement like all the modern big-inch racing machines you have ever seen, the engine climbing the rev band in that leaping gait as the tires hunt for traction, find it, lose it again for a millisecond, then find it until they are locked in.'

The small-blocks were meanwhile blown out to 350 cubic inches through a stroke increase, giving 300bhp with hydraulic lifters and 350 with solid lifters and higher (11:1) compression. They were still the choice of the majority of buyers, although it must be said that the hydraulic-lifter Mark IVs were equally civilized, and commensurately more powerful.

The '69 was improved in important details as well. The grille bars, formerly bright metal, were painted black (many '68 owners had already done that); back-up lights were moved into the centers of the inboard tail lamps; door handles now worked as they had been intended when designed — you squeezed the flap to open the door, and no longer had to press a thumb button. The adjustable steering-column option remained, but now included a tilt feature. Headrests, now required by law, were added at the expense of visibility (which wasn't required. . .). Inertia-reel seatbelts were standard on the coupe and optional on the convertible. A new option to foil Corvette thieves (more Vettes were, and are, stolen than any other car) was a horn-blowing alarm system; the '69 also had a steering-column lock, but this was an across-the-board item on all GM cars in 1969. Particularly neat was a new windshield washing system in which the water jets were carried on the wiper arms; auxiliary jets also washed the outboard (normal) headlamps at the driver's command.

An extensive facelift occurred on the 1970 model, which had been styled after a showcar called the Aero Coupe; the changes included egg-crate grillework, more pronounced fender flares, a higher and more curving windshield, square parking lights set into grille corners, larger side marker lights and rectangular exhaust-pipe tips. Most of these revisions were for practicality rather than the traditional American trim-shuffle. The fender flares, for example, were built in because the lower body sides of 1968–9 models were subject to stone damage. Actually, there was no need for a grille *per se*, since the Stingray's air intake was underneath the normal opening; but the cavity seemed to look peculiar without it.

Unifying the design, the grille texture was repeated in the front fender vents, instead of the four vertical openings previously used.

Prices also began galloping upward: Corvettes now started at over $5000 for the first time; $5192 for the coupe, $4849 for the convertible. This was largely the result of the cost of meeting the rapidly increasing pile of Congressional mandates. Although GM was working overtime on 'clean-burn' V8s to replace the current range, there was no sign of them in 1970: the top-rated Mark IV now developed 460bhp (gross), a high-water mark that has never been exceeded to date. This was, of course, the cammy, higher-compression, mechanical-lifter version; most buyers specified the 'mild' Mark IV with 390bhp. Certainly, the performance was still there: a typical 0–60 time for the 390 was 7.0 seconds flat; the standing quarter-mile took 15 at about 95mph. But the car remained a hard-riding beast. What with modern suspension technology, there was really no excuse for such characteristics in a full-independent-suspension grand tourer; but they have continued to persist right up to the present day.

Federal mandates also effectively squelched any thought of a new Corvette; emissions limits in particular were a problem, and GM was working double overtime to meet them. The 1971 model was little changed, although detuning was now necessary. The largest V8 was 454 cubic inches but the two versions of that produced only 365/425bhp. Sales had dipped to 17 000 with the 1970 price rises; they rose over 20 000 again in 1971 and broke 27 000 for 1972. The '72 was altered only in detail; it was to be the last Corvette with chrome front bumpers or a removable backlight, regulations forcing the abandonment of both. One could easily comprehend what regulations were doing to performance by looking at the 1972 engine line-up. The high-performance 454 (designation LS-6 in 1971) was scrubbed, leaving only the 'civilized' LS-5 but, as horsepower was now being measured in net terms, it seemed low at a mere 270bhp. The Society of Automotive Engineers net standard was closer to true bhp, about thirty per cent less than SAE gross.

The 1972 Corvette was the end of the beginning for the fourth-generation cars: significantly facelifted in 1973, it would run on yet for another decade, but mechanically it would be quite different, oriented more towards luxury than sport. It is appropriate at this point to look at competition, where the fourth-generation cars were — not to put too fine a point on it — outstanding.

The AC Cobra went out of production in 1967 (unlike GM, Shelby could not cope with the Federal mandates and switched his attention to the Ford Mustang). Corvette's SCCA road-racing rebound was almost instantaneous: in 1969, Tony DeLorenzo took the A-Production SCCA championship in a Mark IV, while Allan Barker held the B-Production title with a 350 — the first SCCA wins since 1962. Barker remained the unchallenged B class winner through 1972; his car was then taken over by Texan Bill Jobe, who led the class in 1973—4. At the 24 Hours of Daytona in 1972, DeLorenzo and Don Yenko finished an astonishing fourth overall and first in the GT class.

One of the most successful Stingray compaigners in these years was John Greenwood, whose Mark IVs won the SCCA A-Production championships in 1970-1. Jerry Hansen's Stingray ousted Greenwood from the Class A title in 1972, but John then teamed with TV comedian Dick Smothers to bring a Corvette home first in the GT class at Sebring's 12 Hours in 1972. At Le Mans, Greenwood was the fastest GT qualifier, and led that class until a blown engine forced him to retire.

The age of emissions controls and safety mandates hampered the Corvette's performance but success did not desert the marque. The Stingray won A-production titles from 1973 to 1978, B-Production from 1976 to 1979, and every B-stock Solo II (autocross) championship from 1973 through 1979, with the exception of 1975. Vettes also scored high in Trans-Am road racing, Greenwood running first overall in 1975 (Corvettes were 1-2-3 that year). Greg Pickett's wildly modified racing Stingray won the T/A/A Category II in 1975, although Babe Headley was a distant second to Bob Tullius's Jaguar in Category I. The following year, Category I also fell to the Corvette, a Stingray driven by Gene Bothello outlasting the factory-backed Tullius Group 44 Jaguar. Pickett finished second in 1970's consolidated series, and Eppie Wietzes was point leader in 1981. Not bad for what some said was now a boulevard sports car!

The revamped '73 model set down a new formula for the next 5 years. Responding more cleverly than most to the mandated 5mph bumper regulations, Mitchell's stylists produced a steel-braced, urethane plastic bumper finished in the body color. Fender extractor vents were cleaned up; the trouble-prone flap hiding the windshield wipers was dropped in favor of a GM-modern extension of the hood, which covered the wiper arms when not in use. Other changes included radial tires for the first time, and the option of cast-aluminum wheels. The engine line-up was little changed from 1972. More sound insulation was applied, and chassis mounts made of a combination of rubber and steel to provide both rigidity and noise suppression. The '73 was a quieter car than any Stingray that had gone before and, with the performance age vanishing, that seemed appropriate: sales broke 30 000 — only the second time that had happened — and remained at least that high throughout the decade.

The 'soft bumper' treatment worked so well up front on the '73 model that it was applied to the back of the '74: a neat, sloping shape with inset tail lamps and license-plate bracket. It was this model, too, that saw the final, seemingly irrevocable end to high performance; it was the last car available with a big-block V8 and genuine dual exhausts, and the last to run on leaded fuel.

On the positive side, automatic '74s had the excellent new M40 three-speed, and all used three-point lap/shoulder belts. The traditional handling option was called the Gymkhana Suspension, and cost a mere $7. But it consisted of very hard springs and shocks and, although it was effective on smooth roads, it was pure hell on daily-driver cars.

In 1975, there came another break with the past: the Corvette convertible made its last appearance. Once commanding the lion's share of sales, the ragtop had declined as more and more customers ordered air-conditioned coupes. Better than half Corvette production had factory air by 1972 and soft-top models garnered only 4629 sales in 1975. Electronic ignition put in its first appearance, and small bumper extensions with black pads were added front and rear.

While rumors continued to circulate about an all-new, mid-engined Corvette patterned after Mitchell's swoopy Aerovette showcar, management opted to stay with a design that had become, like Porsche's 911, a classic in its own time. There was scarcely reason to change a car that sold this well — and sell it still did. From 1976 to its final year of 1982, the Vette averaged well over 40 000 customers per annum — astonishing in view of America's new interest in efficiency and fuel economy. The best year was 1979, when 53 807 buyers ordered Corvettes despite a second fuel crisis, the temporary but worrisome reappearance of gas-station lines and another big jump in prices. The 1976 and 1977 models represented the nadir (Nader?) of de-fanged Chevy sports cars; Vettes were little changed in appearance, their solitary 350 V8 offering 180bhp (net) in standard form, 210 optional.

There was life in the old body yet, although just barely. 'We had to do something special for 1978,' Bill Mitchell remembered, 'and it was damn hard to do'. Mitchell, his retirement in sight, was looking for valedictories and he desperately wanted Chevrolet to adopt the Aerovette, which would have been a splendid production car. But other priorities stood in the way: GM was risking all on a rapid downsizing of its entire fleet and an eventual conversion to front-wheel drive on all models save the specialty Camaro/Firebird and Corvette. This was first evident with the downsized 'A' bodies of 1977: a major risk that paid off. GM intermediates were downsized the following year, and the radical X-body family of front-drive compacts appeared in 1979. Styling was told to do what it could with the decade-old Stingray body. It did.

The 1978 Silver Anniversary Corvette (the Stingray name was dropped again that year) was a sensational facelift, a dramatic fastback roofline with a huge backlight, giving unprecedented visibility and the line flowed smoothly into the 1974-designed back end. Cargo space, as a result, increased markedly, although the failure to tool hinges for the backlight, which would really have opened up the space below, indicated how tight was the budget.

Other changes on the 1978 model were small but important: redesigned interior door panels with door handles housed in the armrests; larger, squared-up housings for the speedometer and rev counter to match 1977's restyled center console gauges; a much larger fuel tank (24 rather than 17 gallons). Lift-out roof panels were offered in glass or steel, and the seatbelts were fitted with inertia reels. Chevrolet put the most aggressive tire possible on the '78 in the shape of HR60s (225R/60–15) which marginally improved handling; the rock-hard Gymkhana Suspension option remained available, priced at $41. Two special models were offered during the year: a Silver Anniversary Corvette in a novel silver/gray duotone color scheme and a replica of the car that had paced the 1978 Indianapolis 500. Demand for the latter was high, and several conversions were made up to meet it; a few buyers rashly offered dealers as much as $30 000 to own one. The St Louis plant, working triple-overtime now, actually turned out 6200 Pace Cars, a remarkable achievement, making this the most successful instantly collectable 'replicar' in history.

With St Louis working at higher capacity than it had ever anticipated, few changes were made during 1979–81. The '79s all had lightweight bucket seats borrowed from the 1978 Pace Car Replica; both engines carried the L82-type twin-snorkel air cleaner, and the base V8 gained 10bhp. The final-drive ratio was lowered from 3.08:1 to 3.54:1 in the interests of low-end performance. Incidentally, these cars would still cover 0–60mph in 8–9 seconds and cruise happily all day at well over 100mph — so the loss of performance was relative. There was also, although few people realised it, a five-speed gearbox, called the 4+1 Quick Change. Developed by drag racer Doug Nash, this aftermarket item cost $1000; it carried a split mag-alloy case for quick changes of gearsets and straight-cut spur gears for strength and low friction. Despite the lower final-drive ratio, the Quick-Change increased an otherwise stock Corvette's top speed from 115 to 130mph — and influenced the factory's own forthcoming five-speed.

Seeking incremental gains in economy to help Chevrolet meet government corporate average fuel economy (CAFE) regulations, engineers replaced steel frame and differential components with aluminum in 1980, reducing curb weight by 250lb. A new engine option was the smallest V8 since 1961: 305 inches, a 180bhp powerplant borrowed from the Camaro. Front and rear spoilers, integral with the bodywork, previously optional, became standard on the '80 models, along with air conditioning. But on entering the cockpit, Corvette drivers were nonplussed by an 85mph speedometer! Temporarily this was mandated, but speedos have since begun being honest again. Prices were higher than ever, starting just under $14 000.

More weight was shaved in 1981, but dieting now required very sophisticated tricks. One was a new reinforced-plastic transverse rear spring replacing the steel one, saving 33lb. Others were thinner glass — a dubious sacrifice of strength for lightness — and stainless-steel exhaust manifolds. GM's first Command Control electronic emissions-monitoring system gave precise fuel metering and governed the lock-up of the automatic transmission's torque converter clutch. This improved fuel economy and helped Chevy meet CAFE regulations.

Underlining GM's now established faith in the Corvette was the shift of manufacture in 1981 from St Louis to a new factory in Bowling Green, Kentucky. This change presaged the long-promised, and by now long-overdue, fifth-generation Corvette, being readied for introduction in 1983. Meanwhile, Bowling Green built 25 407 copies of what *Road & Track* accurately labeled, 'truly the last of its series. . .a transition car [with a] new drivetrain in the old body'. Powered by the old engine with new Throttle Body fuel injection on a brand new chassis-frame, the '82 was the first Vette since 1954 available only with automatic.

Celebrating the end of a long, successful run was the 1982 Collector Edition, built only to order and carrying special vehicle-identification (VIN) numbers to ward off counterfeiters. All CEs came with a handsome silver-beige metallic exterior, darker paint 'shadows' on hood and body sides, bronze-tint glass roof panels, cast-aluminum wheels, silver-beige cloth/leather interiors and special cloissone emblems. A prediction of things-to-come was the CE's frameless, lift-up back-light, an item Mitchell had wanted on the 1978 production cars. Exactly 6759 of the 1982 models were Collector Editions; they can be told easily by their VIN prefix: 1G1Y07 (as opposed to 1G1Y87 on standard 1982s).

It was a fair ending to a long story, magnificent proof that the vehicle proudly titled America's only sports car had successfully weathered the worst that government, the safety lobby and assorted Arabs with their fuel monopolies could dish out. Despite all this, we still had a Corvette that could do 125mph and return 20 miles per gallon — a combination of performance and economy that had seemed beyond the limits of achievement 10 years before. It led to the exciting fifth generation, which was better yet — and better by a long way.

Best Vettes

1969
Mark IV 427

Our stable of milestone Corvettes has thus far included only small-block models; it could hardly be complete without an example of the hairy Mark IV. We chose 1969 because, while almost identical to the 'pure' original 1968, it was improved in many details and better built. We opted for the mightiest version of the Mark IV because, like Everest, it's there.

You'll know it's there the moment you twist the ignition key, let alone when the thrust of 460lb ft of torque rockets you to 60mph a split second after the flash-shift to second gear, sending you on to a standing quarter-mile in 14 seconds, by which time you're doing 100mph. This is a typical performance when equipped with the 'acceleration' axle ratio of 4.11:1; take-off is more sedate with lower numerical ratios, but who needs them? The 435bhp Mark IV, with its aluminum heads, mechanical-valve lifters, triple carburetors and 11:1 compression ratio was designed mainly for going out and committing *acceleration*.

At the same time, the big engine (which cost $400 extra at the time and is worth about $3000 extra on the collector market today) is perfectly tractable from 1000rpm. It can be lugged along in fourth gear at silly speeds, in a fashion belied by its rough idle. The clutch is surprisingly light in these cars: except for a little chatter as it's engaged you would never imagine it's linked to such terrifying torque and horsepower.

Of course, at high speeds or low, the 435 provides a cacophony of noise — valve clatter, fan roar, a rorty snarl from the big dual exhausts — to remind you what dwells under the hood. At the 6500rpm red line, this racket builds to a soul-satisfying crescendo, accompanying your shift from second to third past 75mph, or from third to fourth a hair shy of the quarter-mile. Fuel consumption, *driving conservatively*, averages 10mpg. The tank holds only 20 gallons, and wringing 200 miles out of a tankful requires the kind of driving one is not likely to do in this sort of Corvette. But this is an ideal world where you are very rich and can buy all of the stuff you want.

There's another point in its favor, one elaborated upon in the foregoing chapter: this monster *handles*. Chevrolet made handling its most important goal in the fourth generation, and by most measurements they achieved it. Naturally, the suspension has to be very stiff to handle the torque: *Road & Track* actually

Best Yettes

suggested that stiff-wall tires were preferable because the power could collapse radial sidewalls! 'So what you get in the 427 is a hard-riding car, and when the surface really gets rough its willowy frame-and-body construction rattles, squeaks and groans so much it may scare you even though the independent rear suspension does prevent the car from skittering sideways too badly on corners,' *R&T* continued. 'What the car *is* designed for is going fast on a smooth track, and for this it can be bettered only by. . .mid-engine cars.'

The vented four-wheel disc brakes are, by the way, entirely up to the performance potential; road testers found no fade at all in multi-stop tests from high speeds and the proportioning valve to the rear brakes could be adjusted to balance braking and thus to retard lock-up during panic stops.

Add to all this performance and handling Zora Arkus-Duntov's deft detail improvements to the '69 — more spacious interior, a stiffer frame and tighter body, but no change in the smooth and elegant Dave Holls styling — and you come up with perhaps the most desirable Corvette of the fourth generation. If you feel that the Corvettes of the 1970s became gorpy looking and slower in comparison, you have a lot of company: what better representative then, than the '69 435? One other thing; that year Chevrolet called it a Stingray again. That counts for something, too.

Best Vettes

1969 CORVETTE L36 SPECIFICATION

ENGINE

Type	Big-block cast-iron block and heads and five main bearings
Bore	4.250in
Stroke	3.75in
Displacement	427cu in
Compression ratio	10.25:1
Valve gear	Two angled valves per cylinder operated by single camshaft mounted in centre of vee, via 'Porcupine' pushrods and rockers
Fuel system	Single Rochester four-barrel carburetor
Maximum power	390bhp at 5400rpm
Maximum torque	500lb ft at 3400rpm

TRANSMISSION

Type	Four-speed manual
Ratios	1st 2.52:1 2nd 1.46:1 3rd 1.88:1 4th 1.00:1
Rear axle ratio	3.080:1
Body/chassis	Two seat coupe or convertible fibreglass body on welded box section steel ladder frame

SUSPENSION

Front	Independent with double unequal length wishbones, coil springs, telescopic shock absorbers and anti-roll bar
Rear	Independent with single transverse leaf spring and trailing arms, telescopic shock absorbers
Steering	Recirculating ball
Brakes	Discs front and rear, fronts ventilated, 11.75in dia, 461.2sq in swept area
Wheels/tyres	15in × 8in steel wheels with F70 ×15in crossply tyres

Best Yettes

1969 CORVETTE L36 SPECIFICATION
continued

DIMENSIONS AND WEIGHT

Length	182.5in
Wheelbase	98.0in
Width	69.0in
Track	58.7in front
	59.4in rear
Height	47.4in
Weight	3390lb Coupe
	3304lb Convertible

PERFORMANCE

0–50mph	5.5secs
0–60mph	6.9secs

Standing quarter miles 15.0secs

Top speed 136mph

Fuel consumption 11mpg

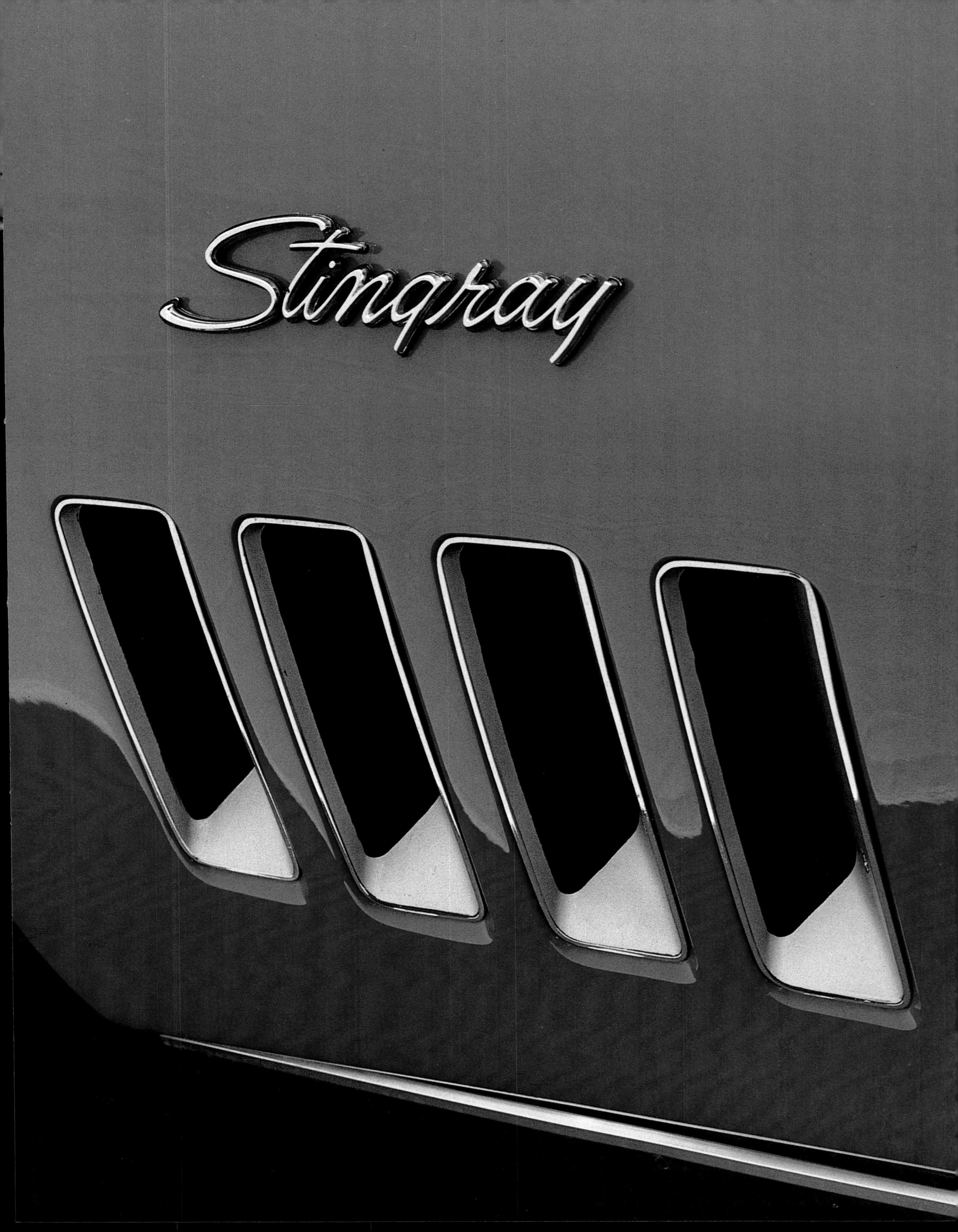
Stingray

PAGE 129 The Corvette generation that was born in 1968 were known as Stingrays rather than Sting Rays, one of the more curious, if least significant, changes.

LEFT Fastest of all the '68 breed was the L88 option with the 427cu in V8 in 435bhp tune, complete with alloy cylinder heads. At $947.90, however, the L88 was an expensive option only taken up by 80 people as the performance gain did not warrant the extra cost.

ABOVE Far rarer than the L88 was the ZR2 of 1971, only 12 of which were sold, with the 425bhp

454cu in engine. The interior is just as others of its generation with a straightforward array of instruments but a center console encroaching even more on driver and passenger.

FOLLOWING SPREAD The 'coke bottle' styling is particularly clear in these views of one of the comparatively few Corvettes to have made it to Great Britain.

PAGES 134/135 That slim-waisted design remained constant, but each year held styling variations such as the two lower square mesh grilles which denote a 1970 model.

FACING PAGE Top of the tree in the 1970 model year was the LT-1 which was powerful enough for the wide F70 × 15 Goodyears on 8-inch rims to be a very sensible option.

ABOVE How much power? The solid-lifter LT-1 version of the 350cu in produced 370bhp.

FOLLOWING SPREAD Apart from the merit of putting more rubber on the road, the $42 option of white-letter tyres filled those wide wheel-arches to perfection.

ABOVE By 1978 the Corvette was 25 years old and to celebrate a Corvette was used as the pace car for the 1978 Indy 500, enabling Chevrolet to produce the pace car replica. Although it was an extra $4000 over the standard model, and mechanically identical, 6502 were sold.

RIGHT The Corvette's flirtation with turbocharging was limited to non-production cars and the Turbo Vette 3 shown on the following spread used this alloy version of the 351cu in V8 suitably strengthened to take the strain of turbocharging via its Garrett AiResearch TO4 turbo. But with the normally aspirated engines producing so much power the turbo route seemed pointless.

ABOVE By the start of the 1980s yearly styling changes were minimal.

LEFT Impressively bathed in street lighting, a classic white '78 model.

FOLLOWING SPREAD End of an era: 1982 was the last year for this generation, and to mark the fact Chevrolet produced the Collectors' Edition with lift-up glass hatch, special alloy wheels and the distinctive gold finish, all of which helped it become the first Vette to break the $20 000 barrier.

PAGES 148/149 The current style of Corvette made its debut as a 1984 model (there was officially no '83 model) and was soon seized on by Callaway Engineering who produced a twin-turbo conversion. This is the '88 model with twin intercooled Rotomaster turbos, a power output of 382bhp and a top speed of around 190mph.

Chevrolet's aim with the '84 model was to challenge and beat the best sports cars in the world. To that end the Corvette was given a new frame and sophisticated independent suspension using beautifully detailed cast alloy components. Both front and rear springs were fiberglass, and the body was a form of unitary construction. Although the '84 carried on the original design concept of thirty years before (front engine, rear drive fiberglass two seater), it was as modern as any of its rivals. Power came from the injected 350cu in V8 producing 250bhp at 4300rpm and giving a top speed of 140mph.

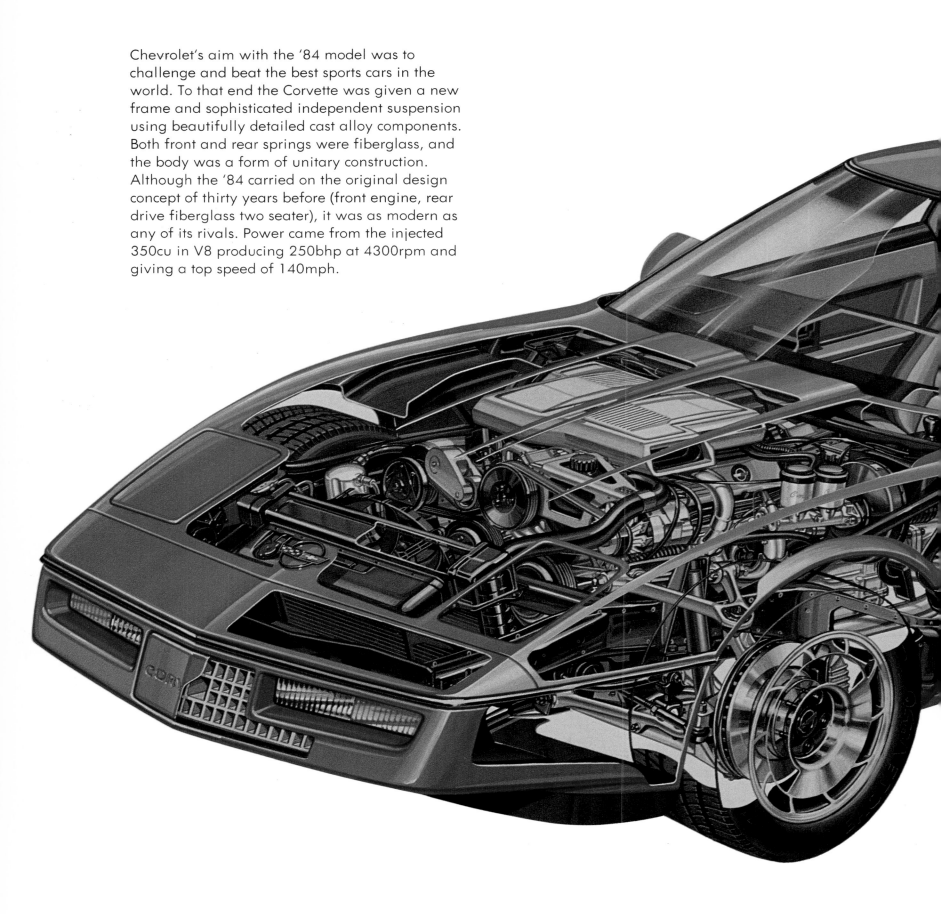

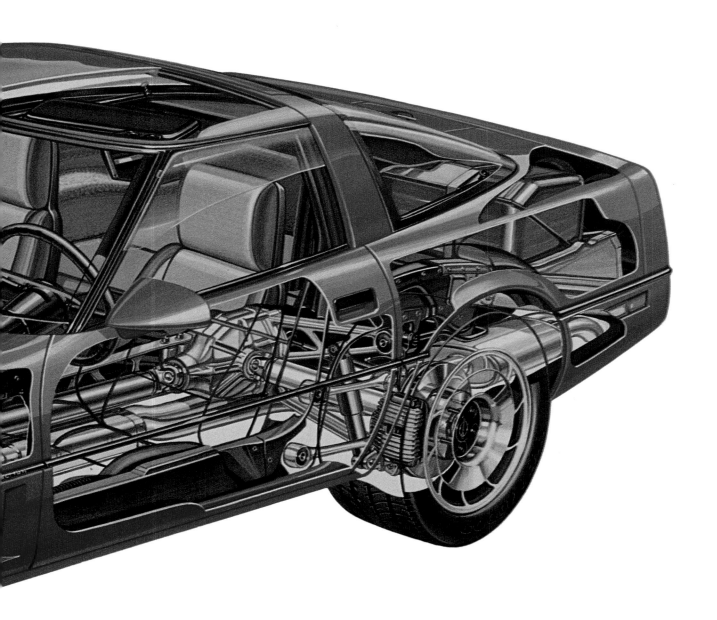

With a drag coefficient of 0.34 the '84 Corvette was quite as slippery as this shot taken inside GM's Aerodynamic Laboratory indicates. Nevertheless, the car's reduced frontal area did make it more aerodynamically efficient.

A
CONTINUING
AFFAIR

1984 – 1989

MOST Detroit cars take 3 years to gestate; the 1984 Corvette (introduced as an '84 in February 1983, and skipping the '83 model year) took 5. Work began virtually the day in July 1978 that GM decided *not* to go ahead with Bill Mitchell's radical rear-engined Aerovette. Corvette development, decided the company in that year of dim prospects for the industry, would be evolutionary rather than revolutionary. Along with the Camaro/Firebird, the Corvette would retain a front-engined, rear-drive layout, with a big-inch V8 engine indefinitely.

While this was a compromised, committee decision, its validity can hardly be questioned a decade later, with 6 years' worth of the latest and best Corvette behind us. At the time, however, it caused many GM watchers to speak darkly of the Corvette's future, or to shake their heads about the corporate bean-counters.

However, all that was before they saw the result, which was the perfect combination of tradition and state-of-the-art technology. Two men whose names have since become enshrined in Corvette lore led the design to its brilliant

conclusion: Jerry Palmer, head of Chevrolet Design Studio 3, and Dave McLellan, who headed the engineering team.

McLellan recounts the history of the venture from Aerovette to '84. The Aerovette, he said, was not practical, given the market requirements Chevrolet had to meet. 'When you get to a high-performance car that carries two people and has some kind of creature comforts, the mid-engine gets very tough to deal with. Nobody had — and still hasn't — come up with a mid-engine design that is a fully marketable car. All these mid-engine cars are not without their difficulties.' Similar reasoning caused GM's dropping of the Pontiac Fiero.

Around the time the Aerovette was being dropped, Porsche produced its 928, which opened many eyes. Here, at a time when the world-wide trend was to four and six-cylinder engines and engineers spoke of mid-engined locations as the wave of the future, was a long-time producer of rear-engined fours and sixes offering a front-engined V8.

'As we analyzed the old Corvette,' McLellan

continued, 'a lot of things, we felt, were right. That was reflected in its performance in the marketplace. We look at this new Corvette as an ultimate performance statement by Chevrolet. What I mean by that is, in all respects that are important to a Corvette, the car needs to be king of the hill. If it's worth doing, it's worth doing better than anybody else. With the old Corvette, we had kind of let things slip a little bit.'

Once the engineers (not accountants, sales types nor product planners) convinced top management to retain the traditional formula, they were allowed wide latitude to perfect it — in fact, they were given a clean slate to design the new Corvette from the ground up. The first benchmark was actually a tire, the Pirelli P7. Although Goodyears rather than Pirellis would be fitted in production, the P7 was a fine standard. 'Much of the design was done around that tire,' McLellan said. 'We brought Goodyear in early and gave them the specifications, and they worked hard on it. We're very pleased with the results. The tires have been trouble-free and have better hydroplaning performance than previous tires.'

Then there was that all-important consideration for new designs of the 1980s: aerodynamics. The fourth-generation Corvette had (despite its swoopy lines) an unacceptably high coefficient of drag, nearly 0.50. In fact, in its early design stages it was even worse than that, proving actually inferior to the third-generation Sting Ray in wind tunnel tests. By 1982, this had been reduced to 0.44, which was still far too high but, by the time the new Corvette project began, General Motors had built its own wind tunnel at the Warren, Michigan, Tech Center allowing unprecedented concentration on aerodynamics. 'This car was really designed in the tunnel,' Dave McLellan remarked. The 1984 model had a Cd of 0.34, 'and we know how to get it down to a 0.31, or even 0.30 in honest production trim'.

Another point on which both engineers and stylists were adamant was the continuation of glass-reinforced-plastic construction. As David McLellan pointed out, 'It has the ability to absorb minor impacts, and is nearly as light as aluminum; it doesn't rust or corrode'. Indeed, the only reason we don't see more cars made entirely of fiberglass, he added, was because it was more expensive; yet 'you are seeing more and more use of reinforced plastics'.

McLellan is always at pains to praise his colleague, Jerry Palmer, who he said 'fine-tuned the design', adding that he was glad Palmer was in charge by the time the new car was being styled. 'The only way we really got our act together on this car was by waiting until Bill Mitchell retired. The previous car was never really accepted outside the US. Export requirements were taken into consideration very early in [the new] design, so changes were kept to a minimum.' Export models are produced ready-to-ship alongside North American versions at the Bowling Green, Kentucky, plant; McLellan was proud that they did not have to be retrofitted with special equipment, and were exported to a variety of countries including Britain, France, Belgium, Germany, Sweden, Austria, Italy, Switzerland, Japan and various Middle Eastern states.

Jerry Palmer was as different from his flamboyant predecessor Bill Mitchell as a Porsche is from a Corvette; in fact, some people would say Palmer is more suited by temperament to the Porsche. Quiet and soft spoken, Palmer states his truths without exaggeration or colorful hyperbole, and never knocks his competition, domestic or foreign. Yet he managed one of the most remarkable feats in recent Detroit history with the '84 Corvette: retaining a look and feel that long-time devotees would recognize, while working to state-of-the-art engineering parameters.

Like McLellan, Palmer started from a very small given base, the engine and transmission. 'We literally laid out the package with a clean sheet of paper. [All that was set down was the] need for additional ground clearance.' Palmer is also, obviously, a team player. 'Dave [McLellan] knows enough about what we do to understand or challenge. . . . I would say Chevrolet was very creative in helping us achieve the package we wanted. To come up with the idea and make it look good is one thing; to make it work is another. There is more integration between [design and engineering] than there was [before]. We have a better understanding of what has to be done to make the product people are demanding.' Palmer has made light of the famous criticisms levelled at the new car by his former boss who, he said, complimented him on everything but the back end. 'If Bill were running the studio I don't think the Corvette would be a lot different. . . . It was, after all, a philosophy of "form follows function". Bill always approved of that.'

Palmer pointed out that the ultimate shape of the '84 was predicated on its wider stance. Although its wheel arches were flared as before, the sides were smooth and flowing rather than thin in the middle and bulged at each end; the beltline was one continuous line running uninterrupted from the A pillar to the Kamm-style tail with its traditional dual tail lights. The last mentioned were inset and without screw heads – both dictates of the wind tunnel. A full perimeter rubbing strip wrapped right around the car, serving visually to link the tops of the front and rear bumpers.

The body chosen was a Targa-type coupe, with a single, removable roof panel in the body color; later, as an option, buyers could order a scratch-resistant, tinted acrylic panel. This component had been well thought out; it had a special storage compartment built into the top of the cargo platform, and a special wrench to remove it, hampering theft. Dropping the traditional T-bar lost some rigidity, but this was more than made up for by the tremendous strength of the new 'unibody' construction.

With the determination to retain a traditional V8 front-drive layout, one might reasonably ask why so much had to change. The answer lies partly in the fact that the fourth-generation car it replaced went back to 1968 – and its design dates back even farther, to 1965. In the halcyon days of 1965, with no real competition, the Corvette could get by with a cramped interior, poor visibility and a driving position that resembled sitting in a bathtub. A dozen years later, there was a lot more competition, from Europe and Japan. The designers actually started from what they called the T-point, or the location of the seated driver's hip joint. They raised this by 1 inch and moved it back an inch, improving the former characteristics immensely. The higher seating position, coupled with larger, 16-inch, wheels, allowed more ground clearance, which was another goal of the exercize. The wheels were initially an option to the standard 15-inchers but, shortly after production began, they became a mandatory option.

The aforementioned P7 Pirelli radials were a benchmark for the engineers, but only because of their technology; Goodyears, as mentioned, were being developed specially for the '84 as standard equipment. These tires were rated for speeds in excess of 130mph and had what Goodyear called Gatorback tread – large horizontal gaps perpendicular to the tread pattern (which looked like the back of an alligator) adopted to prevent hydroplaning by channeling water out from under the wide footprint. The wide wheels (8.5 inches front, 9.5 rear) so complemented the handling that previously impossible g forces were routinely recorded by road testers. 'The roadholding is so advanced,' said Car and Driver, 'that we recorded the highest skidpad lateral acceleration – 0.90g – ever observed with a conventional automobile by this staff. That figure practically trivializes the previous high-water marks. . .generated by such exotics as the Porsche 928 and assorted Ferraris.'

The clean-slate approach naturally produced a new, steel backbone chassis, the spine a C-section beam carrying the driveshaft. The unit weighed less than the old perimeter-type ladder frame, contributed to the spaciousness of the interior, and allowed the exhaust system to be routed under the driveshaft instead of taking the conventional route alongside. A sub-structure or 'birdcage' was welded to the frame which formed the windshield, door frames, rocker panels, cockpit walls and front subframe, and carried a U-shaped frame at the rear which served as base for the frameless, lift-up rear window. An extension for the back bumper and a front-suspension mounting unit were also bolted on. Galvanized to retard corrosion, this structure formed the base upon which the fiberglass body panels were attached, and meant the '84 was the first Corvette to employ a unit body-frame.

Fully redesigned, the new suspension consisted of a five-link rear set-up consisting of upper and lower longitudinal links mounted between the hub carriers and the body, twin lateral strut rods connecting the differential with the hub carriers and the familiar transverse, reinforced-plastic leaf spring plus U-joined halfshafts and rear-mounted tie rods. The rear leaf spring was now repeated up front, where it was mounted between the two lower A-arms, along with an anti-sway bar; a 5mm thicker bar was part of the Z51 handling package. The steering also changed, from recirculating ball to rack-and-pinion. The rack was mounted well forward to improve precision and to provide high-effort power assistance for better control at high speeds. The standard steering ratio was 15.5:1, but the Z51 package raised it to 13:1. All steering wheels had tilt and telescope features.

Motive power was probably the most familiar part of the mechanical specification: the well proven L83 5.7-liter (350 cu in) V8 with twin throttle-body electronic fuel injection and Cross-Fire induction with dual ram-air intakes. Rated output was 205bhp at 4300rpm; torque was 290lb ft at 2800rpm, both figures being fractionally increased from 1982. The combination of effective new suspension and that engine gave a safe 140mph top speed and 0–60 times of under 7 seconds, with the standing-start quarter-mile only 15 seconds. That made the Corvette one of the five or six fastest production cars in the world.

Stopping the beast was also a major concern.

Oversize, vented four-wheel disc brakes, hydraulically assisted, were designed for Corvette by Girlock, a US offshoot of the British Girling Company. Light and powerful, they featured one-bolt (for quick-changes) pads, rubbing 11.5-inch rotors. No road tester was ever known to criticize the Corvette's ability to stop, as well as go.

The transmission was totally new. Not only was the standard unit a four-speed again (automatic had become standard in 1982); it was a kind of dual unit, a normal four speed attached to a second, planetary, gearset controlled by the Computer Command electronics. The auxiliary gearset sat at the rear of the transmission and engaged through a hydraulic clutch in all ratios except first, providing an overdrive reduction of 0.67:1 in each of the top three gears, improving flexibility and economy. The overdrive could be locked out with an override switch, and turned itself off under hard acceleration. The final-drive ratio was 3.07:1 with a 3.31:1 ratio available for improved acceleration. The formerly standard GM 700-R4 automatic four-speed transmission, with its lock-up torque converter clutch, was officially optional, although delayed shipping of the four-speed caused most early '84s to be fitted with the automatic.

One design goal lost along the way was lightness; the engineers had wanted the '84 to come in with a curb weight under 3000lb, but had to settle for 3200lb unladen; this was still about 250lb less than the '82, however. It was accomplished mainly by the substitution of aluminum or plastic sheet-molding compound (SMC) for steel wherever possible without losing strength. The standards were high, mainly because Chevrolet had every intention of building a convertible again as well as the coupe. Dave McLellan, who thought of convertibles as 'throw-backs', criticized the compromises implicit in a two-model philosophy. 'I can't tell you how many pounds are tied up in open design, but it's a lot. Structural integrity is important. For light weight, coupe construction is the way to go. . . .

We wanted an open feeling, in contrast with the De Lorean. That's the ideal of a closed-in car.'

The interior of the fifth-generation cars was a total break with the past; the trouble was that not everybody liked substitutes for plainly visible and comprehensible white-on-black instruments. The designers felt different, however, deciding an all-electronic, digital/analog panel was the only way to go, and provided such a display for every engine function. A switch in the center console allowed the driver to monitor different functions, such as consumption, trip mileage, fuel range, engine temperature, oil pressure, voltage and water temperature.

The console also carried air-conditioning controls and the audio controls. Optional at a staggering $895, but worth it according to audio connoisseurs, was the GM-Delco/Bose sound system. Seats were high-back buckets with the first reclining mechanism in Corvette history. Cloth upholstery was standard, leather optional, and Lear-Siegler seats available on order for the truly committed, which had electric controls for seatback cushion position, backrest angle, and lumbar support (via inflatable/deflatable bladders).

Despite all the care and clean-slate thinking that had gone into the fifth generation, the production cars brought several disappointments along with all their fine performance and technological advances. These can be summarized by a word that had long haunted the Corvette over the years: it still seemed unsophisticated. The 0.9g handling was there, all right, but at the expense of ride, and the ride/handling combination still failed to approach state-of-the-art designs by the Europeans and Japanese despite all the team's work. The stiff, Z51 handling suspension was virtually unacceptable on the street. 'It's a balls-out calibration that ruins the car for day-to-day use,' said Car and Driver's Don Sherman. 'Really bad pavement sent its wheels bounding, and even minor bumps threw the car off on momentary tangents.' In addition, the '84s were noisy, seriously so. 'Exhaust and road noise are loud at anything above idle speed, though the exhaust settles down when cruising in O/D,' reported Consumer Guide.

It is a curiosity that in Europe, where paving technology seems far advanced over North America, high-performance cars are nevertheless capable of a razor-edge balance between ride and handling that makes them particularly desirable in the US and Canada, where pavements are torn apart by broad climatic changes. Yet in North America, where one would think they'd learn such things, the same kinds of cars rarely display such a judicious balance. The Corvette has continued to suffer from these complaints, and it is sad that such a beautiful, responsive and reliable performance sports car should not be, at the same time, truly comfortable.

There were no external changes on the 1985 model, which arrived at the normal time in the autumn of 1984. Cross-Fire Injection was, however, replaced with Tuned Port Injection, a multi-port system which alone increased output by 25bhp to 230 net. It also gave the typical Corvette a genuine 150mph capability, and reduced its acceleration times. The '85 also rode slightly better. Chevrolet engineers had changed the spring rates on both the conventional and Z51 suspensions, widened the front tires to 9.5 inches to match the rear, and replaced the conventional tube shocks with gas-pressurized Delco Bilsteins.

Corvette production had been bubbling along at high levels in the final years of the fourth generation: 1979 had been the record year, at 53 807. The new '84 chalked up 51 547 sales, misleading, maybe, as the '84 model year lasted 18 months. The improvements wrought for 1984 did not come without charge and, between '82 and '84, the starting price had climbed from near $18 000 to around $24 000. The 12-month sales rate was only 34 000, and for the 1985 model year, which was normal length, Corvette sales were 39 729. This dropped to around 35 000 in 1986 – despite the advent of the first convertible Corvette in 11 years.

This was somewhat ironic since the 1986 convertible, improved in many ways, was by many yardsticks the finest Vette in history. All the structural work went into the ragtop, and for 1986 the new model proved tighter than the coupe, which certainly was a switch.

The work on the open car included a forward frame cross-member with K braces connecting the cross-member to the frame rails, steering mounts and front torque box. A cross-beam was positioned behind the seats and an X-brace under the mid-section; the seat-back riser was a double steel panel and the door-latch mechanism was strengthened. The following year, as everyone predicted, all these improvements were applied to the coupe to good effect.

The convertible top retracted into its own hatch, as it had on Corvette ragtops before it. This model had its own suspension, with lower recommended tire pressures, a small decrease in ride height and deflected-disc Delco shocks. The improvement in ride comfort was worthwhile, and did not cost much in handling.

Both the coupe and convertible had a new and worthwhile Bosch-designed anti-lock braking system, improved anti-theft systems, and freer-breathing dual exhausts. All of the 7264 convertibles built for the 1986 model year came with 'Indy Pace Car Replica' decals to identify them with the Corvette convertible that paced the 500 that year, but these were supplied with, rather than affixed to, each car. Most of them, happily, stayed unaffixed as you would hope on a car that cost over $30 000, or some $5000 more than the coupe. The Bosch ABS II anti-lock braking system was a logical development in a car of this class, and essential given the rapid adoption of ABS on rival high-performance machines. Integral with the four-wheel disc brakes, ABS relies on electronics to control braking force at any wheel, whenever that wheel is about to lock up. Whether or not it is crucial under normal street conditions, it certainly renders an already good braking system one step closer to perfection.

It appears likely at this early date that the convertible will improve its share of Corvette production, but probably to little more than one-third of the total, which it reached in 1987 with 10 625 for the model year against 20 007 coupes. It will never be the dominant model that it was in the Sting Ray years, but it is good to know that throw-backs are still available, for those who think, with Ogden Nash, that progress was all right once, but has gone on for too long.

The 1987s were a matched pair, since the coupe had gained the extra stiffening of the convertible and in the process had become the tightest Corvette of the new generation. Changes for '87 were evolutionary, and mainly mechanical: roller hydraulic lifters were selected to reduce friction loss, rocker-arm covers had raised rails to prevent oil leaks, while spark plugs were moved closer to the centers of the combustion chambers to improve burning capabilities and to retard knock. Fuel economy improved a bit and power was up slightly, improving by 10bhp, to 240bhp net, but the obvious improvement was in pulling power. A hefty gain of 55lb ft gave the already potent powerplant a massive 345lb ft. If you think this encouraged lead-foot habits, you're right, but the fifth generation had never been as economical as its planners had hoped. Typical mileage for the '87 was 16–18mpg.

An interesting and useful option (although pricey at $325) was an electronic tire pressure monitoring system, which warned the driver of a drop of as little as 1psi below a preset minimum in any individual tire. This shocking occurrence would light up a warning lamp on the dashboard. The trick was accomplished by pressure sensors mounted at each wheel, beeping radio signals. Tiny transmitters did this job, powered by generators that converted mechanical energy from the moving wheels into electrical energy. There were no wires, spinning or otherwise, and the entire unit weighed less than two pounds.

There were still few subtleties about the Corvette, as Rick Popely and Chris Poole wrote in

Consumer Guide's *Auto '87*: 'The 5.7-liter provides blistering acceleration, a top speed of over 150mph, and cruises around town almost effortlessly (though with a deep exhaust note). Corvette's stiff suspension and huge tires give it amazing cornering ability that lets you accelerate around 90-degree turns. . .the standard anti-lock brakes do the job safely, even on wet or snow-packed surfaces. However, slippery roads are bad news for the high performance tires, so you'll lose a lot of traction for acceleration and cornering. Bumpy roads are bad news also, since there's little give to the suspension, so the occupants and the body absorb most of the road shock. . . .Chevrolet designed the Corvette to be a race car first, a street car second.'

A race car first? Wasn't this Corvette designed with all-new parameters built around sporting luxury? Yes, but the designers were allowed plenty of latitude, and the designers were car buffs. Whenever it came to a choice between total performance and road-going comfort, performance won hands down. And, while not overtly into racing itself, GM gives enormous technical assistance to those who do.

Chevrolet has closely liaised on an IMSA (International Motor Sport Association) prototype powered by a turbocharged V6, with a Lola-designed, hyper-streamlined machine that resembles (not exactly accidentally) the production Corvette. Competing in the Camel GT series and driven by Doc Bundy and Sarel Van Der Merwe, the car is raced by Hendrick Motorsports under the sponsorship of GM Goodwrench, service arm of the parent company.

Corvette chief engineer Dave McLellan says that Corvette is in the racing game to stay. 'There's the overall statement on Chevrolet performance we're making with the Lola turbo V6 GTP car project. That's a joint venture between ourselves and Ryan Falconer, who is doing the turbocharged V6 motors. We did the aero work on the car [which will be] a testbed development tool to wring out the vehicle system as a competitive prototype vehicle. Then it's up to various private racers to take replicas of that car and turn them into successful racers. We're doing the part of that venture that we do best, which is supporting engine development and doing the aerodynamic development.'

At the opposite end of the racing spectrum in SCCA Showroom Stock and Trans Am competition, fifth-generation Corvettes have carried on the tradition of their forebears. The Showroom Stock class national championship has been Corvette property since the '84 arrived; SS Corvettes have also placed first in such races as the Mid-Ohio and Willow Springs enduros, and the SSGT class.

The presence of a turbo V6 in the IMSA prototype has given rise to speculation that something along those lines may be entering production as a sixth generation. Some Chevy sources have hotly denied this but McLellan stands above the fray: 'We're not going to see that in the short run [but] if we can see a V6 turbo that would outgun the V8 and had fuel economy and what other benefits it would need to be viable, we would consider it. [Still,] we have such a damn good engine in the small-block V8. Its evolutionary progress outstrips anything we can demonstrate in a competing alternative. That engine in NASCAR form is putting out over 600 horsepower and we are continuing to evolve the engine.'

Chevrolet is often asked whether a sixth generation is imminent, especially when it reels off showcars like the stunning, mid-engined 1986 Indy — a return, in a way, to the Aerovette idea, but advanced 10 years. So far, the powers that be insist that no big change is in the offing. 'As long as fuel prices do not become outrageous, and all other things being equal, the current configuration has a long potential life,' McLellan concludes. 'If there is some dramatic shift in consumer demand, we'll have to reconsider what we're doing.'

The Indy was certainly a reconsideration; Chevrolet Division chief engineer Don Runkle calls it 'a work in progress'. It is also very international, being designed by Chevrolet, with Lotus suspension (and strong developmental input by that firm) and assembled by the Italian company Cecomp (which also produced the Lotus Etna). The first car was a show model, but a running prototype called CERV-III was produced in late 1986.

Chief mechanical attraction of the Indy, aside from its swoopy styling by Jerry Palmer, Tom Peters and Tom Reiss, is its transverse V8 Ilmor engine of only 2.6 liters sporting double overhead cams, twin turbochargers and intercoolers and 600 horsepower. In the Indy, the engine used pump fuel, rather than alcohol as provided for CART racing and the Indianapolis 500. Underneath were full-time four-wheel drive, with front/rear/mid differentials connected by driveshafts, and four-wheel steer, with the rear wheels moving in an arc of up to 10 degrees. Equipped with the production anti-lock braking system, the Indy used its individual wheel sensors to govern acceleration as well as braking. If any wheel spun faster than the others, the system quickly snapped its disc caliper on and off, slowing it down; if too much torque was applied, the computer likewise backed off the power. It will be interesting to see how this new technology affects drag racing.

All mechanical innovation, however, was obscured by the Indy's styling. 'The words "soft" and "sensuous" come to mind,' wrote John Lamm in *Road & Track*. 'The Indy leaves behind the wedge-shape, folded-paper school of exotic car design.' Bill Mitchell would have been proud.

The Indy was pretty impressive inside, too, thanks to beautifully shaped, form-fitting bucket seats with rounded contours and a rakish 40-degree back angle. To get in, one swung the doors up and forward. Occupants confronted an array of controls and individual CRT monitors on both doors, the driver's main controls being confined to stalks under the steering wheel. This space-age interior is credited to Chevrolet designers Julian Carter and Patrick Furey.

The Indy gave us a look into the future, but the future is still a long way off. What they have been doing meantime is punching out more of the traditional package — if the fifth generation can already be called a tradition. The 1988 model was again a near-clone of its predecessors with the same subtle but important underskin improvements. Wheel design was changed slightly, and a 17-inch wheel option added, complete with monster P275/40ZR-17 Goodyear Eagle GT radials. The standard tires were P255/50ZR-16, rated for speeds over 150mph. The suspension was revised front and rear to give better control under hard deceleration.

More work was done on the brakes, which used larger, thicker, rotors and dual pistons up front (the 17-inch wheels were supplied with even larger rotors). Aluminum cylinder heads of a revised design were added to improve breathing, and a slightly revised camshaft raised output to 245bhp. Horsepower gains have been incremental over the last few years, but if they keep going up at this rate they will keep the Corvette on top of the competition.

In a company as large as General Motors, it's quite remarkable that the Corvette has managed to remain true to itself and its public for more than 35 years, despite the ups and downs of the economy, the politicians (both in Washington and Detroit), the concern for the environment, the Middle East and the Greater East Asia Co-Prosperity Sphere.

You just have to give credit to the Corvette's designers and engineers for their loyalty to the original idea. No other Detroit car has been blessed with such uniformly car-besotted people, who insist that the Corvette should remain above all an enthusiast's automobile.

Give credit too to its loyal customers: it is they who have made this story possible. Their loyalty is summarized by a typical reply to a typical question. Asked how they like their last Corvette, chances are they'll answer: 'Haven't bought it yet.'

Best Vettes

1989 ZR1

When it comes to adding a fifth-generation car to our mythical stable of classic Corvettes, two choices stand out from the rest: one of the very first '84s off the line, from back in early 1983; or the very latest and greatest. Astonishing as they were, the '84s were subject to a certain amount of well known teething troubles, so we'll opt for the latter and recommend to your attention the long-awaited ZR1.

Heart of this maximum-performance '89 is a 350-cubic-inch V8. Ho-hum, you say. The good ol' L98 350 has been around for donkeys' years. But wait: Chevrolet calls this engine the LT5. It is somewhat different.

There is for example a surfeit of valves (thirty-two), camshafts (four), fuel injectors (sixteen) and induction systems (two). The primary injection system engages under normal conditions, with eight relatively small injectors. The secondary system, with eight more high-flow injectors, comes on when a key is turned in a special console switch. Ancient 'ad hacks', who wrote about 'unlocking the power' of the Tucker Torpedo or Hudson Hornet, would be fascinated by this setup.

Designed by Lotus, the engine is built by Mercury Marine, the outboard-motor people. Surprised? You shouldn't be. The Stillwater, Oklahoma, company is one of the world's most qualified builders of precision-cast aluminum, which is used in the LT5 block, heads, intake manifold, cam covers, pan and front cover. Chevrolet adds that Mercury is an ideal builder, since it is used to small production runs and hand-assembly; LT5s will be built at the rate of about 50 to 200 per week.

This mighty engine develops close to 400bhp net, making the ZR1 (which is fully equipped with every possible suspension, tire and braking device in the 1989 inventory) the most hairy-chested street Corvette in the history of the fifth generation. We can expect 0–60 times close to 4 seconds flat, and 12-second standing quarter-miles at 110mph+, with a top speed of over 175mph. The L88 born again and then some?

The ZR1 will, however, be a perfectly tractable car at ordinary speeds, thanks to the split personality of its two-stage fuel injection system. And, of course, it will also enjoy the latest round of improvements Chevrolet has laid on for the seventh model year of its generation.

Chief among these is a lovely six-speed manual gearbox designed in

Best Vettes

tandem by McLellan's Corvette Engineering Group and the famous ZF Company in Germany. Replacing the long-running 4+3, the new transmission will offer ultra-short first- and second-gear ratios at one end, coupled with two overdrive gears at the other. Officially dubbed the ML9 transmission, this should prove ideal for the ZR1, since the LT5 has a torque output of 425lb ft and comes with a hydraulically actuated 11-inch clutch. It also features computer-aided gear selection: an automatic shift from first up to fourth if coolant temperature exceeds 120 degrees F, or speed falls by between 12 and 19mph or the throttle-position sensor reads less than 35 per cent travel. CAGS, as they call it, will therefore not make itself known, unless intervention is needed. A good idea.

The 1989 Corvette also features electronically controlled Selective Ride, available with the ML9 gearbox and Z51 performance suspension: soft (Touring), conventional (Sport) and Z51-level (Competition) settings may be selected using a console switch. Not three but eighteen suspension settings are possible, since six different automatic shock absorber settings are computer-selected within each mode, the damping effect becoming harder as speed increases.

These factors considered, the 1989 Corvette must be considered the most sophisticated and highly developed Corvette in our five-car stable of classics, and the ZR1 the most impressive performer as well. The only thing about it that gives pause is the thought of one's son asking for the 'key to the console'.

1989 CORVETTE ZR1 SPECIFICATION

ENGINE

Type	Quad-cam V8 with alloy block and heads, wet liners and five main bearings
Bore	3.9in
Stroke	3.66in
Displacement	350cu in
Compression ratio	11.25:1
Valve gear	Four valves per cylinder at 22 degrees included, angle operated by two chain driven overhead camshafts per bank of cylinders with variable valve timing
Fuel system	Direct Fire electronic sequential fuel injection
Maximum power	385bhp
Maximum torque	N/A

Best Yettes

TRANSMISSION

Type	Six-speed ZF manual
Ratios	1st 2.68:1 2nd 1.80:1 3rd 1.29:1 4th 1.00:1 5th 0.75:1 6th 0.50:1
Rear axle ratio	N/A
Body/chassis	Two seat fibreglass/plastic coupe body with integral perimeter frame 'birdcage' chassis forming unitized body

SUSPENSION

Front	Independent with double unequal length forged alloy wishbones, transverse monoleaf epoxy/glass spring telescopic gas shock absorbers and anti-roll bar
Rear	Independent with adjustable five-link system: upper and lower trailing arms, lateral arms, tie rods, transverse monoleaf glass/epoxy spring, telescopic gas shock absorbers and anti-roll bar. Selective Ride Control gives three ride/handling settings
Steering	Rack and pinion
Brakes	Ventilated discs front and rear, 11.5in dia. Electronic anti lock
Wheels/tyres	17in × 9.5in 'handed' allow wheels with P275/40ZR 17 Goodyear Eagle ZR40 radial tyres

DIMENSIONS AND WEIGHT

Length	176.5in
Wheelbase	96.2in
Width	71.0in
Track	59.6in front 60.4in rear
Height	46.7in
Weight	3257lb

PERFORMANCE

Top speed 180mph (estimated)

THE ASSEMBLY LINE

ST LOUIS FACTORY The 300 1953 model Corvettes were built essentially by hand at Chevrolet Plant Number 35 near Flint, where fiberglass panels from the Molded Fiber Glass Body Company in Ashtabula, Ohio, were glued together in rough wooden jigs. There was a crudeness to the process: '53s show obvious signs of hand-laid glass cloth techniques, and many differences exist from car to car. All such cars were considered prototypes; plant 35 served to establish methodology and, once that was sorted, production was transferred to a General Motors Assembly Division plant on Union Boulevard, St Louis, Missouri.

The last car left St Louis on Friday, 31 July 1981, 698 314 Corvettes later. It had grown from a hole in the wall operation to a factory occupying an entire city block, employing 1450 workers with an annual payroll of $20 million. St Louis' capacity was said to be 30 000 Vettes a year, but Chevrolet began stretching this in the '60s; by the time it closed, the plant was turning out over 40 000.

Despite ever-increasing numbers, St Louis was proud that it applied more hand work to its cars than any other GM plant in the country. It began with the receipt of MFG's body panels into an enclosed booth, where the occupants were dressed in astronaut-like suits and breathed piped-in air. Here the panels were blasted with tiny balls of steel shot on the panel edges and joining surfaces, creating a rough finish for bonding.

Construction began with the underbody — the largest single fiberglass panel — mounted on a moving jig, so workers could add plastic and aluminum reinforcements. Further along, men with cake decorators (a nickname for glue dispensers) spread lines of bonding material on the join surfaces. When panels were pressed together, a chemical heating reaction occurred, leaving a bond even stronger than the individual panels.

Complete bodies were then placed on a slow moving line where more men in protective clothing and hoods sanded and smoothed the body seams. Because this was done at least partly by hand, with everything from files to circular sanders, no two Corvettes were ever exactly alike. One major difference from a conventional plant was the way large panels were moved around — they were so light that they could be carried into position. Again, this was done by hand.

The painting process was laborious, consisting of repeated sanding, spraying and baking. The work began with a dry sanding and hand-rubbing of putty to fill cracks and imperfections, and was followed by a first coat of primer. After baking at 200 degrees, the bodies were wet sanded and a second coat of primer applied. Then they were baked again. The wet-sanding process occurred at least twice, sometimes more if the standards weren't met; lacquer was then applied. After another baking (at 180 degrees) and a second coat of lacquer, the body was hand polished to a high gloss.

Finished bodies were placed on a motorized production line where windshields, dashboards and exterior chrome were applied — again, entirely by hand. On a separate chassis line, following individual testing, the engines were dropped in using a chain hoist. Finished chassis then met finished bodies, and the attachment bolts were tightened. Finally, the cars travelled along another assembly line where interior trim, insulation and options were fitted.

By 1979, the historic St Louis plant was no longer suitable for Corvette production. Chevrolet did not expect to sell *more* Corvettes, so capacity was not the main problem. GM President Thomas A. Murphy said that clean-air regulations were affecting decisions; in order to comply with controls on paint fumes, the plant would have to devote four times as much space to a redesigned paint operation. Even for more conventional car production, GM invested $100 million in improvements to meet regulations, and for better efficiency.

Compared with the output of other plants, St Louis' Corvette line was infinitesimal. At the peak of output in 1979, cars were being built at the rate of ten an hour, or 180 per day in two 9-hour shifts. After the Corvette moved out, light-duty Chevy and GMC trucks were built, at the rate of thirty-five per hour.

BOWLING GREEN PLANT General Motors maintained that the vacant factory in Bowling Green, Kentucky, into which the Corvette moved starting with the 1982 model, was one of many choices. Unofficially, according to the *Louisville Courier-Journal*, it was selected because Kentucky — a state that works hard on bringing in new industry — successfully wooed GM through tax and loan assistance, and the city by a 20-year lease on the highly suitable factory, which it owned.

Bowling Green was opened in 1969 by Chrysler Airtemp, and later operated by Fedders, to produce commercial air-conditioning systems. Located three miles east of the center of town, the building boasted 565 000 square feet of floor space, a figure GM doubled during renovation work. Plenty of room is left: the factory is situated on 200 acres just off Interstate 65, and on a spur of the Louisville & Nashville Railroad.

The first Bowling Green Corvette was a beige 1981 model. It rolled out of the plant on 1 June 1981 and was presented by a local dealer to a women's club, which raffled the car.

The former air-conditioner plant was completely renovated, and its employees trained in the latest assembly technology. Initial employment was 1150, and the 1982 payroll was $48 million (which, compared to St Louis' 1979 figures of 1450 and $20 million, shows how much salaries had risen!). The production rate was fifteen Corvettes per hour on a one-shift basis, which contrasts favorably with St Louis's volume of ten an hour using two shifts. A second shift is operated when orders require, often in the fall of the year after the new models have gone on sale.

Compared with St Louis, Bowling Green is highly automated and computerized. Computers are relied on to check emissions, with separate standards for California and the other 49 states as well as the EEC and Canada; to regulate energy use; to check tooling for wear and to keep track of countless quality and production-related details. However, because of the Corvette's fiberglass construction, some processes closely resemble those of the former plant.

Completed bodies now enter a space known as the clean room through tight, Corvette-shaped openings, where they are prepared for final finishing. Workers in the clean room wear disposable coveralls that look like surgeon's gowns, with their clothing, hair and shoes also covered to keep dust out of the air and off the drying paint. Bodies travel suspended from a three-rail carrier while chassis are carried on a ground-based line called the Tow-veyor. When the two assemblies are nearly complete they are carefully aligned and married. The chassis is released from the Tow-veyor, and the car is carried overhead on the three-rail carrier to receive last-minute items such as wheels and shock absorbers. Then it returns to the ground for testing and delivery to the shipping dock.

Demand for Corvettes since the fifth generation began has not been high enough to test Bowling Green at its maximum, but the emphasis remains on quality. 'Everything that goes through this plant undergoes a quality inspection,' said planning administrator Larry Mendenhall. 'The tooling, the machinery, the entire facility is brand new, and it's all for quality. All the assemblers check their own work individually — they know if they did it right. They've had many hours of training in all areas of whatever job it is they are doing. Then, there are 111 inspectors, who check to make sure that everything is done just right, from raw material to finished Corvette.' If the quality of recent Corvettes is any indication, Bowling Green is soundly fulfilling its role.

PAGE 169 Corvette concept cars from two eras — the Indy of 1986 with its quad-cam V8, four-wheel steer and four-wheel drive. Below it is the Aerovette of 1978 that was on the verge of becoming a production car.

PAGES 170/171 The Indy's control center — an extension of the Corvette's standard electronic displays.

PAGES 172/173 The body style of the current generation of cars has been left almost unchanged; visual differences lie in details like these alloy wheels for the '88 model.

PAGES 174/175 Hi-tech luxury in the '84 model. The power seats adjust all ways and the electronic display between the graph speedo and rev counter is programmed to display different functions at the touch of a switch.

ABOVE A radical departure from the traditional pushrod V8: the all-alloy LT5 engine used in the '89 ZR1. Developed in conjunction with Lotus of England it features four cams, 32 valves and produces 380bhp from 350cu ins.

ABOVE When the current shape first appeared, the car was available as a coupe only.

FOLLOWING SPREAD The discrete rear badge is a little misleading; the LT5 engine went into production in the '89 ZR1.

PAGES 180/181 The cast alloy sculpture covers a sophisticated intake system in the LT5 engine; only two of the four valves per cylinder operate at low engine speeds, opening up to feed more fuel as speed rises.

PAGES 182/183 The 'LT5' in flight.

The Corvette's separate front and rear deformable
sections allow styling changes to be made
without altering the main body panels, as well as
performing their main function of crash
protection.

FIBERGLASS
FANTASY

THE MARKETING
OF THE
CHEVROLET CORVETTE

MOST talented advertising copywriters in America who really *like* cars have probably sent a job resumé at one time or another to the Lintas Campbell Ewald advertising agency in Warren, Michigan, even though success could mean moving to Detroit.

From the copywriter's point of view, if you're going to write car advertising, you might as well write about one of the most exciting cars in America — the Chevrolet Corvette. To have a Corvette ad in your portfolio has always been something special.

Lintas Campbell Ewald, Chevrolet's only national ad agency since Chevy started building automobiles, has been blessed by the presence of the Corvette in the Chevrolet line-up because the mere opportunity to work on Corvette advertising has attracted a lot of very talented people to the Chevrolet account over the years.

Barney Clark, David E. Davis, Jr, William Jeanes, Bruce McCall, Jim Wingerson, Jim Ber-

nardin, Jim Ramsey, Roger Honkannen and Jim Hartzell have all passed through the agency while one of their number, H. Kyle Given wrote a book on the subject published by *Automobile Quarterly* entitled *Corvette: Thirty Years of Great Advertising.*

The chosen few who worked on Corvette were a little different from the rest. Corvette advertising has always been a labor of love, one which was usually afforded special status within the hallways of the agency. And more often than not, the work that emerged was truly exceptional, satisfying not only the reader's technical curiosity about the product, but also that area of the brain that makes you yearn to break free and feel the wind in your face and the road rushing beneath, all to the thrum of a throaty V8.

What follows are some highlights of the Corvette advertising campaign over the past 35 years — a long running eulogy that has echoed and fostered the car's special image.

One automobile has defined the sports-car experience for America better than any other: the Chevrolet Corvette. As the oldest two-seater nameplate in America, as well as the oldest nameplate in the Chevrolet stable, Corvette has a rich tradition, molded not only by the car's unique qualities, but also by an advertising campaign spanning more than 35 years.

The unofficial theme attached to the Corvette over this period is *America's only true sports car*. It is an appropriate slogan, given the exclusivity of the Corvette in the American market over the years. There have been other American two-seaters to rival the Corvette, but none has survived in its original form. The 1956–7 Thunderbird grew larger in 1958 and has been a personal luxury car ever since. The Bricklin and De Lorean came and went, as did the Pontiac Fiero. More recent rivals are the Buick Reatta, Cadillac Allante and Chrysler Maserati but, while these cars have a sporty character, they were never designed to be true sports cars.

The Corvette is different, and it has consistently met all the performance definitions of the sports car. Powered since 1955 by the Chevrolet small-block V8 engine and benefiting from a continued string of engineering changes led by Chief Engineer Zora Arkus Duntov, the Corvette quickly established itself as a brash sports car with a unique American character, thanks to its size (large for a sports car) and its thundering V8 power.

Corvette advertising, coupled with image-building TV shows like *Route 66*, where Todd and Buzz packed their belongings and pointed the nose of their Corvette west every week, helped mold the image of the Corvette into a *bona fide* symbol of the American dream.

When the Corvette was introduced in 1953, it literally *was* a dream car, being a production version of the prototype that debuted at the January 1953 General Motors Motorama, at that time an annual affair in New York to give each GM division a chance to show off its new concept vehicles. But while all the other 'dream cars' from the first Motorama were destined to become museum pieces, the first Corvette rolled off the production line a scant six months later.

The early Corvette advertising was fairly straightforward, dwelling on its exclusivity and its sports-car qualities. In keeping with previous events the themeline in 1954 heralded: *First of the dream cars to come true.*

But Corvette advertising didn't start to get really interesting until 1955 when Barney Clark joined Campbell Ewald, Chevrolet's advertising agency. A former car-magazine editor, Clark was not only knowledgeable, but also a passionate and brilliant copywriter.

'The challenges of those early days of Corvette advertising were, however, very similar to the challenges of marketing the car today,' said Clark. 'When the Corvette was introduced back in 1953, we were faced with how to position it against the great cars of its day – Jaguar, Aston, Porsche, Ferrari, and so on.

'But the biggest hurdle wasn't knowing what to do, but how to deal with a mentality both within the agency and at GM that didn't relate to selling performance cars. Getting some of those people to understand cars was like trying to get a group of homosexuals to design a girl,' said Clark.

Despite the obstacles, Clark persisted and created what many regard as one of the best automobile ads of all time entitled *Child of the Magnificent Ghosts*. It began (see facing page):

No Chevrolet ad ever read like that before. And Clark admitted much later that he thought 'Ferrari,' but wrote 'Corvette' during those days.

But as time went on, Clark and the Corvette faithful in America were getting a lot more to believe in, thanks to the efforts of Zora Arkus Duntov. Duntov and Clark became allies and friends and, while Duntov took control on the engineering side, Clark became the marketing advocate for the kinds of enthusiast engineering programs Duntov was pushing.

Years ago, this land knew cars that were fabricated out of sheer excitement. Magnificent cars that uttered flame and rolling thunder from exaust pipes as big around as your forearm and came towering down through the white summer dust of American roads like the Day of Judgment.

They have been ghosts for forty years, but their magic has never died. And so, today they have an inheritor – for the Chevrolet Corvette reflects, in modern guise, the splendor of their breed.

It is what they were: a vehicle designed for the pure pleasure of road travel. It handles with a precision that cannot be duplicated by larger cars – and it whistles through curves as if it were running on rails.

You can watch a Corvette in action and imagine some of the elation it offers. But who can tell you about the cyclone sound of that 195-horsepower V8 engine, or the fantastic surge of acceleration that answers every ounce of throttle pressure?

Who can make you feel what it is like to drive a car that has more on hand – in road-holding, acceleration, stopping power – than you'll virtually ever use? You'll have to try it for yourself. And we'll take particular pride in showing you the car that is the true child of those magnificent ghosts – the V8 Corvette!

'Things weren't easy,' Clark said. 'You'd think Chevrolet at that time regarded racing as the work of Satan. And they didn't know what kind of performance potential they had with the small-block V8.'

But if the advertising was any chronicle, a lot of good things were beginning to happen by 1956. Then, Duntov drove a camoflaged '56 Chevy sedan up Pikes Peak in record time. And Dr Dick Thompson took the 1956 Sports Car Club of America C Production national championship.

Ads in 1957 announced the introduction of fuel injection and new outputs of one horsepower per cubic inch of engine displacement. In 1958 and 1959, the continued refinement of the chassis and engine dominated the advertising, which was building a case for the Corvette as a lifestyle all to itself.

Barney Clark left Campbell Ewald in 1960 to write Lincoln Mercury and, later, Ford advertising. Before leaving Campbell Ewald, however, he wrote one of his favorite ads, a teasing taunt with sexual overtones directed at those who had not experienced a Corvette: *For ten seconds, try to imagine what owning a Corvette would be like. . . You're close, but it's better than that!*

Clark was replaced at Campbell Ewald by a young copywriter named David E. Davis, Jr. Davis is now Editor/Publisher of *Automobile* magazine but has also served as Editor/Publisher of *Car and Driver*, and Creative Director on the Chevrolet account at Campbell Ewald.

Many advertising critics feel that it was Davis who, along with art director Jim Bernardin, produced one of the best strings of sports-car advertising done by anyone: ads like *Some guys have it tough*, which showed a guy and a girl in a white Corvette convertible pointed toward the ocean on a Malibu beach as the sun is setting.

The copy read:

Corvette owners are not necessarily the most carefree people in the world, but there are moments when every Corvette driver must think himself thrice blest. Here's a car that, more than any other, has an uncanny ability to erase the day's cares and woes and whisk its driver far, far away. Turn on the key, engage first gear and step on it: Goodbye office, hello better things in life. We'll make no attempt to analyze the chemistry of such a phenomenon; it's all blurred by things like the feeling of the wind on your face, the sound of the Corvette exhaust, the cyclone surge of a truly great V8 engine. We will be more than happy, however, to direct you to your nearest Chevrolet dealer to sample a Corvette. Look at it, sit in it, drive it, and you'll find that we haven't exaggerated a bit. We couldn't exaggerate these things if we tried.

'The ultimate compliment I ever received from a Corvette ad,' said Bernardin, 'was when a dealer called me up and told me a customer brought in a copy of *Some guys have it tough* from a magazine. He then bought the car on the spot.'

Other ads such as *Breaking the boredom barrier; You only think you're not an enthusiast; Farewell lackluster transportation* and *Aficionados are made, not born* all helped sell the notion of the Corvette as an emotional purchase that could add spice to the life of the owner.

'In the early '60s, the advertising process was a lot simpler, without elaborate lighting techniques or expensive models,' said Bernardin. 'We used a lot of guys with bald heads as models and we didn't pay them $1000 per hour.' Davis himself was used as the model in the 1961 ad, *Glory road*. Another 1962 ad featured the daughter of Chevrolet Chief Engineer Ed Cole as a passenger in one of the cars.

The 1963 model year saw the debut of the stunning new Corvette Sting Ray and the debut of a new Corvette copywriter named Bruce McCall. Some of McCall's best work was seen the following year in 1964 with ads like *Phantom of the opera coupe* and *Clip along dotted line*.

McCall went on to join the staff of *Car and Driver* and later formed the McCaffrey McCall

Advertising Agency, taking on the Mercedes-Benz advertising account. He also wrote some classic humor books.

After McCall left, a writer named Jim Ramsey took over and produced some classic ads in 1966. One of these was *Why men leave home*. The visual shows a romantic couple looking out at the profile of a Corvette Sting Ray coupe from the shelter of a cave, on a lazy Saturday afternoon.

Equally provocative was the ad from the same year, *The day she flew the coupe*. Here, we see a stunningly attractive woman, standing in the middle of a stream, her soaking-wet clothes clinging to her body as she munches on a peach. The car is posed seductively behind her, and the copy reads:

> *What manner of woman is this, you ask, who stands in the midst of a mountain stream eating a peach?*
>
> *Actually, she's a normal everyday girl except that she and her husband own the Corvette coupe in the background. (He's at work right now, wondering where he misplaced his car keys.)*
>
> *The temptation, you see, was overpowering. They'd had the car a whole week now, and not once had he offered to let her drive. His excuse was that this, uh, was a big hairy sports car. Too much for a woman to handle: the trigger-quick steering, the independent rear suspension, the disc brakes — plus the 4-speed transmission and that 425 HP engine they had ordered — egad! He would have to teach her to drive it some weekend. So he said.*
>
> *That's why she hid the keys, forcing him to take public transportation. Sure of his departure, she went to the garage, started the Corvette and was off for the hills, soon upshifting and downshifting as smoothly as he. His car. Hard to drive. What propaganda.*

And what an ad! Another particularly memorable ad for the big-block L88 427-cubic-inch engine was: *Flight 427, now departing through gates 1, 2, 3 and 4*.

The 1967 model year saw a shift from the emotionalism of earlier years to a gutsier straight-forward approach typified by ads such as *Deuces Wild*, showing tri-power two-barrel carburetors on the big-block 427. Other ads such as *Wolf in wolf's clothing*, and *Disappearing machine*, touted the pure kick of big-block V8 power.

1968 saw the introduction of an all-new body style, while the ads continued with the macho approach typified in ads such as *Superiority complex; Perpetual emotion machine* and *The car that talks back*.

191

The 1969 campaign once again touted the exclusivity of the Corvette in the American marketplace with this headline: *With this beautiful exception there is no such thing as a true American sports car. '69 Corvette.* Another ad that year stated: *You don't have to beware of any substitutes. There aren't any.*

If the 1960s represented a coming of age of the Corvette in terms of the car's development and the marketing approach behind it, the '70s represented a regression, reflecting the effects of the energy crisis and excessive governmental regulation in the American auto industry.

Horsepower was on the decrease and the advent of unleaded fuel meant that engines had to be tuned to run on lower octane. During this period, Corvette advertising all but disappeared, with just one pure Corvette ad appearing in each of the years 1971 and 1972, and only two ads appearing in each of the years 1973 and 1974; just one ad appeared in 1975. Despite all this, Corvette sales remained strong, with as many as 46 558 coupes selling in 1976.

In 1977, Corvette advertising came alive again with an ad written by Jim Hartzell, the man who coined the phrase: *Baseball, Hot Dogs, Apple Pie and Chevrolet*, one of Chevrolet's most memorable themelines ever.

The headline was *The role of the dream car in the age of reality* and the copy read:

Dreams.

They sustain us, they spur us. Sometimes they simply help soften the rough edge of our days.

In that noble regard, Corvette has performed with true distinction over the years.

To own such a fabled car as this one day, one time. Now that's a dream that ranks with scaling tall mountains and sailing wide seas.

For most, for sure, it's a dream that remains unfilfilled. But remains, nonetheless.

Corvette, America's only true production sports car. With a shape and a stance and a spirit all its own. A classic cockpit, disc brakes all around, fully independent suspension. And roof panels you can lift off to see the stars.

Our dream car is not without its practical aspects, of course. It has among other things a body that simply cannot corrode. (It's made of fiberglass).

And there are just two seats. One for you, one for her. Does a dreamer need more?

Corvette. Not just a car, an inspiration.

Sweet dreams.

The late '70s Corvette advertising was characterized by ads for the 1978 Indianapolis 500 pace car: *Some of the world's fastest cars will try to keep pace with it.* But perhaps the most memorable aspect of 1978 was Chevrolet's offer of a full billboard size advertisement of the Twenty-Fifth Anniversary Corvette, measuring 10ft by 21ft, arriving in twelve 'easy to assemble' sheets. The cost of this was $11.50.

Corvette advertising was still sparse going into the '80s, with customer interest cautious because of the continued rumors of a new car on the way.

The enduring qualities of the Corvette were brought out in this, the only Corvette ad produced in model year 1980:

In this ever changing world, some things endure.

A fine red wine.

Soft smoke on an autumn evening.

A walk along the seashore.

And Chevrolet Corvette.

Now 26 years young. And still America's only true production sports car.

But endurance can live side by side with improvement. For 1980, air conditioning, power windows, and Tilt-Telescopic steering are standard equipment.

There's a bold, new front-end design with an integral air dam. A new rear spoiler has been built in and there's a new, lower profile hood. Cornering lights have been added.

The strong tradition of Corvette roadability continues: independent front and rear suspension, four-wheel power disc brakes and steel-belted radial tires, large-diameter front sway bar — all standard.

But beyond the machinery, there is the dream — Corvette and the open road.

For thousands, that dream endures.

The next several years were relatively quiet on the marketing side, as Chevrolet, Campbell Ewald and the rest of the world anxiously awaited the all-new car which debuted in 1983 as a 1984 model.

And when the day finally came, it was a historic one for the Chevrolet Corvette advertising campaign in that it contained the very first Corvette television commercial.

A 90-second epic entitled *Never Before*, its pounding musical refrain uttered, 'You've never seen anything like this before'. And the words rang true, at least when it came to automotive TV commercials.

Shot with a budget reported to be over a million dollars, using high-tech, sci-fi camera and editing techniques under the watchful eye of Director Bob Abel, the commercial literally took the viewer throughout the car, showing everything from the instrument panel to the stereo system. A driving sequence even duplicated the feeling of the tunnel on the Grand Prix course at Monaco. The commercial was perhaps more befitting a high-tech fighter jet than a sports car, but was still a commercial that few would forget.

The spot, written and produced by Jim Nichol of Campbell Ewald, won top honors that year at the US Television Commercial Festival.

Besides a TV commercial, the 1984 Corvette was also heralded in a series of multi-page units, dwelling heavily on the performance and technology of the car.

The first of these was entitled, *The exotic American*, with the subhead reading *A new Corvette is born and it will take you places you've never been before*. The inside of this unit touted the car's lateral acceleration in excess of 0.9g on the skidpad and also its acceleration and braking capabilities.

Three other similar units were prepared, each devoted to different aspects of the car's performance. Perhaps the most memorable piece of print advertising from the '84 campaign was a headline requoted from the pages of *Car and Driver*. It boldly read: *Best production sports car on the planet*.

Besides the traditional insertions in car-enthusiast publications, the 1984 Corvette ad campaign also featured a series of technological brag and boast ads in the *Wall Street Journal* which attempted to marry the technology of the Corvette to that contained in other Chevrolet products at the time.

In 1985, Corvette received a big boost in performance thanks to the 'Tuned Port Injected V8', replacing the Throttle Body Injection on the 1984 car. With this major improvement in power output, the advertising that year attempted to answer the question everybody was asking: 'Just how good is the Corvette, compared with the world's top exotic automobiles?' To answer that question, Campbell Ewald rounded up some of the top world-class competitors for Corvette — Ferrari 308, Lamborghini Countach, Lotus Esprit Turbo and Porsche 944 and 928S. The agency then brought in the United States Auto Club (USAC) to certify tests of the cars that were conducted both at Laguna Seca Raceway in Monterey, California and at the GM Proving Grounds in Mesa, Arizona.

Of course, the Corvette emerged as the overall performance winner, coming in first in the categories of braking and slalom; it finished second in lateral acceleration and third in acceleration.

The USAC tests were then recreated for the cameras, which resulted in a series of TV commercials touting the 1985 Corvette as a *World Class Champion*. A three-page gatefold print ad was also created. The headline read, *These European exotic cars all have one thing in common. . .They've all been beaten by America's exotic car. . .Chevrolet Corvette*.

Also in 1985 appeared the first motor-sport win ad for Corvette since *The real McCoy* in 1956. The ad stated *A world-class champion proves it again* and the occasion was the victory of the Morrison Cook Corvette in the 1985 24-hours Nelson Ledges race, an enduro for SCCA Showroom Stock Cars that has become quite a hotbed of manufacturer interest, both in America and abroad. Chevrolet was finally, after all these years, publicizing its involvement in racing.

The following year, the comparison theme with other exotic cars was used again, this time to demonstrate the Corvette's ability to steer and stop on wet pavement. One headline read: *Antilock braking power you can grade on a curve*. A TV commercial was also produced demonstrating the same thing, showing the competition sliding helplessly forward, knocking cones into the air while the Corvette neatly negotiated a turn under hard braking.

On the motor-sport side, the Corvette was selected as the pace car for the 1986 Indianapolis 500. That alone was worth an ad, but equally interesting was the fact that test pilot General Chuck Yaeger was chosen to drive it. Campbell Ewald decided to tie these two heros together in a special tongue-in-cheek ad for the Indy 500 program. The resulting headline read: *Just pace the racers Chuck, don't humiliate them.*

The year of 1987 marked the debut of the *Heartbeat of America* campaign for Chevrolet as well as a memorable TV commercial for Corvette entitled, *Boy and Car.* Written by Pat O'Leary of Campbell Ewald, the spot captured the special feeling that most every red-blooded American boy has had for the Corvette, at one time or another.

It opened under a multi-colored western sky at dusk as a young boy walks out of his house to grab the mail. But something catches his eye out in the distance, a red Corvette convertible, churning up dust as it descends down the hilly dirt road like a triumphant warrior. The look on the boy's face says it all, as he wipes the dust off his brow. The spot then cuts to show the boy projecting himself into the car. The copy read: *If you've got a dream, put yourself behind the wheel of Today's Chevrolet and listen to your heartbeat.* A simple concept, yet it was enormously powerful.

In 1987, Chevrolet was chosen as the featured marque at the annual vintage-car races at Monterey, California, one of the biggest events of its kind in North America. It was a rare opportunity for Chevrolet really to promote its performance heritage, and what better vehicle to do that with than the Corvette?

A special ad for the occasion was prepared by Campbell Ewald. The visual showed Corvette Chief Engineer Zora Arkus Duntov behind the wheel of the Corvette SS race car *circa* 1957. The headline was: *Echoes of thunder. . .at Monterey '87.* The copy read:

Memories fade but the machines live on. . .

They have lain quiet now, testimony to an era, stowed lovingly in dark garages and museums.

But on August 22–23, in Monterey, California, the tarps will come off. Fresh fuel will splash into their tanks. Starters will crank and those faded memories will explode to life with the most memorable sound in motorsports — Chevy thunder. Imagine a blue Corvette SS at Sebring, a bright orange McLaren at Elkhart Lake, a dark blue Corvette Grand Sport at the Bahamas, a white-winged Chaparral at Le Mans.

Come to the Monterey Historic races on August 22–23 and see the great thundering Chevrolets that rewrote the history books and inspired generations of car enthusiasts. You'll also help Chevrolet salute 75 years of high performance.

In 1988, the *Heartbeat of America* themeline continued for Chevrolet, and four Corvette ads were produced, using a unique visual approach. Four well known American automotive photographers — Jim Turcott, Peggy Day, Jim Haeffner and Dick Reed were approached, initially for the 1988 Corvette catalog. They were encouraged by Gene Butera, the Director of Catalogs at Campbell Ewald, to go off and do any sort of photographic interpretation they wished with the car. No art directors from the agency would be allowed to accompany them. This unexpected freedom brought about some very interesting results. So interesting, that Campbell Ewald attached some well known philosophical quotes as headlines and ran them as ads. An example is an ethereal shot of a black Corvette convertible blasting away from the camera. The headline was a Thomas Fuller quote: *There's no going to heaven in a sedan.*

A consistent level of motor-sport advertising for Corvette continued in the 1988 campaign, represented by an ad announcing the newly created Corvette Challenge, a single-model series sanctioned by the Sports Car Club of America for Showroom Stock class Corvettes. The series was created after the SCCA banned the Corvette from the Escort Endurance series after Corvettes won every single race for three years in a row. The subhead of the ad stated: *A car so unbeatable they had to create its own race series: The Corvette Challenge.* The headline then read: *It takes one to beat one.*

Thus far, the Corvette challenge has been a wonderful success, with some of the most competitive racing in North America.

As we enter the '90s, the Corvette's future looks bright indeed. Chevrolet is committed to keeping the Corvette among the very top performing sports cars in the world, with models like the all new Corvette ZR1, powered by a 400-horsepower four-cam, all aluminum V8 designed by Group Lotus.

'America's only true sports car' appears destined to remain so for some time to come and as such has an appeal which transcends differences in incomes, education and profession.

The Vette Owner

The type of person who buys a Corvette has changed as much as the car over the years. When the car was introduced in the '50s, the Corvette buyer was similar to the average Chevrolet buyer in income, education and occupation. In fact, at that time, Chevrolet didn't even separate Corvette buyers out from the mainstream in compiling demographic data, although we do know that in 1964, the first year for which there's data, the median income of Corvette buyers was $12 000.

As the car began to change in the '60s and '70s, so did the buyers, becoming increasingly affluent, better educated and higher on the executive/professional ladder.

This trend has become even more pronounced since the mid '80s, with median income of Corvette buyers jumping by almost $25 000 in 1988, compared with 1984. And with the introduction of the ZR1 Corvette in 1989, which came in at a price close to $50 000, the upward demographic spiral is set to continue at an even higher rate.

In the 1980s, the largest percentage of Corvette buyers were between 35 and 55 years old, quite a contrast to the '60s and '70s, when an average of seventy-five per cent of Corvette buyers were under the age of 35. This statistic would seem to go hand in hand with some of the price increases on the car. People over 55 have never made up more than ten per cent of Corvette buyers, although average age has been climbing, if not steadily. In 1988, it was 39, compared with 30 in 1964, while the all-time low of 26 dates from 1968.

Corvette buyers are predominantly male, but the number of female buyers has slowly crept up over the years, peaking in 1985 with twenty-two per cent of the total. The number of college graduates purchasing new Corvettes has remained near fifty per cent throughout the past 10 years. In the '60s and '70s, that figure was closer to forty per cent. In 1968, the percentage of college graduates plunged as low as thirty-one per cent, the same year as the average age dropped as low as 26 — clearly the '68 had a distinct appeal.

Throughout the '80s, managers/proprietors have composed the largest percentage of Corvette buyers, followed by executives, the unhelpful category of miscellaneous others, sales people and merchants. During the years of the 1970s, for which data is available, managers and proprietors composed the largest buyer segment followed by professional/technical people, sales people, skilled laborers and miscellaneous others. In the '60s, miscellaneous professionals composed the largest segment, followed by skilled laborers. In 1989, the idea of laborers being able to afford a Corvette seems fantastic. But if you're moving America's only sports car up to the level of one of the world's best, if not *the* best, it can no longer be a car for everyman. Still, as our ad survey shows, dreaming was always a strong part of the Corvette mystique.

YEAR-BY-YEAR
PRODUCTION SPECIFICATION

Year	Body	Price	Production
1953	Convertible	$3498	300
1954	Convertible	$2774	3640
1955	Convertible	$2774	145
	Convertible V8	$2909	549
1956	Convertible	$2900	3467
1957	Convertible	$3176	6339
1958	Convertible	$3591	9168
1959	Convertible	$3875	9670
1960	Convertible	$3872	10 261
1961	Convertible	$3934	10 939
1962	Convertible	$4038	14 531
1963	Convertible	$4037	10 919
	Coupe	$4257	10 594
1964	Convertible	$4037	13 925
	Coupe	$4252	8304
1965	Convertible	$4106	15 376
	Coupe	$4321	8186
1966	Convertible	$4084	17 762
	Coupe	$4295	9958
1967	Convertible	$4240	14 436
	Coupe	$4388	8504
1968	Convertible	$4320	18 630
	Coupe	$4663	9936
1969	Coupe	$4780	22 129
	Convertible	$4437	16 633
1970	Coupe	$5192	10 668
	Convertible	$4849	6648

Year	Body	Price	Production
1971	Coupe	$5496	14 680
	Convertible	$5259	7121
1972	Coupe	$5533	20 496
	Convertible	$5296	6508
1973	Coupe	$5561	25 521
	Convertible	$5398	4943
1974	Coupe	$6001	32 028
	Convertible	$5765	5474
1975	Coupe	$6810	33 836
	Convertible	$6550	4629
1976	Coupe	$7604	46 558
1977	Coupe	$8647	49 213
1978	Coupe	$9351	40 274
	Limited Edition	$13 653	6502
1979	Coupe	$10 220	53 807
1980	Coupe	$13 140	40 614
1981	Coupe	$16 258	40 606
1982	Coupe	$18 290	18 648
	Collector Edition	$22 537	6759
1984	Coupe	$21 800	51 547
1985	Coupe	$24 878	39 729
1986	Coupe	$27 502	27 794
	Convertible	$32 507	7315
1987	Coupe	$28 474	20 007
	Convertible	$33 647	10 625
1988	Coupe	$29 955	15 382
	Convertible	$35 295	7407
1989	Coupe	$32 045	
	Convertible	$37 285	

NO 1983 model year

Child of the magnificent ghosts

Years ago this land knew cars that were fabricated out of sheer excitement. Magnificent cars that uttered flame and rolling thunder from exhaust pipes as big around as your forearm, and came towering down through the summer dust of American roads like the Day of Judgment.

They were the sports cars in a day when all motoring was an adventure, and no man who ever saw one can forget the flare of sun on brass, the brave colors and the whirlwind of their passage.

They have been ghosts for forty years, but their magic has never died. And so, today, they have an inheritor — for the Chevrolet Corvette reflects, in modern guise, the splendor of their breed.

It is what *they* were: a vehicle designed for the pure pleasure of road travel. It handles with a precision that cannot be duplicated by larger cars — and it whistles through curves as though it were running on rails.

You can watch a Corvette in action and imagine some of the elation it offers. But you have to put your own hands on that husky steering wheel to taste the full pleasure of really *controlling* a car.

Who can tell you about the cyclone sound of that 195-horsepower V8 engine, or the fantastic surge of acceleration that answers an ounce of throttle pressure? Who can describe the wonderful feeling of confidence and relaxation that stems from true sports car roadability, or the genuine astonishment that comes when you first tap those rock-solid brakes?

Who can make you feel what it is like to drive a car that always has more on hand — in road-holding, acceleration, stopping power — than you'll virtually ever use? You'll have to try it for yourself. And when you drop in at your Chevrolet dealer's, he'll take particular pride in showing you the car that is a true child of those magnificent ghosts — the V8 Corvette! . . . Chevrolet Division of General Motors, Detroit 2, Michigan.

CHEVROLET CORVETTE

THE REAL McCOY

Here is the most remarkable car made in America today — the new Chevrolet Corvette.

Why remarkable?

Because it is *two* cars wrapped up in one sleek skin. One is a luxury car with glove-soft upholstery, wind-up windows, a removable hardtop (with virtually 360° vision), or fabric top, ample luggage space, a velvety ride and all the power assists you could want, including power-operated fabric top* and Powerglide transmission*.

The other is a sports car. And we mean the real McCoy, a tough, road-gripping torpedo-on-wheels with the stamina to last through the brutal 12 hours of Sebring, a close-ratio trans-mission (2.2 low gear, 1.31 second) matched to engine torque characteristics, razor-sharp steering (16 to 1) that puts *command* into your fingertips.

Other people make a luxury car that has much the same dimensions as this. That's not so tough. And the Europeans make some real rugged competition sports cars —and that's considerably tougher. But nobody but Chevrolet makes a luxury car that *also* is a genuine 100-proof sports car.

It's a wicked combination to work out, and we didn't hit it overnight. But you'll find, when you take the wheel of a new Corvette, that the result is fantastic — the most heart-lifting blend of all the things you've ever wanted a car to be.

If you find it hard to believe that one car could combine such widely different characteristics we can't blame you. And no amount of talk can tell you half so much as 15 minutes in a Corvette's cockpit — so why don't you let your Chevrolet dealer set up a road test of the most remarkable car made in America today? . . . Chevrolet Division of General Motors, Detroit 2, Michigan.

*Powerglide and power-operated fabric top optional at extra cost.

PEBBLE BEACH

Production Car Race, Over 1500 c.c.

1st in Class C — CORVETTE
2nd Over-all — CORVETTE

FINISH

The 1956 Corvette is proving — in open competition — that it is America's only genuine production sports car. Extremely stable, with outrigger leaf springs at the rear, 16 to 1 steering ratio and weight distribution close to 50-50, it has demonstrated its ability to corner on equal terms with the best European production sports cars. Of particular interest to the competition driver are the close-ratio manual gearbox, with 2.2 to 1 low gear and 1.31 to 1 second gear; the two rear axle ratios of 3.70 to 1 or 3.27 to 1; the power-to-weight advantage of the Corvette's glass fiber body and the special racing brake lining, now available at Chevrolet dealerships.

Mainspring of the Corvette's performance is, of course, the fantastically efficient 4.3-litre V8 Chevrolet engine. Holder of the Pikes Peak stock car record, heart of the Corvette that set a two-way American mark of 150 m.p.h. at Daytona Beach last January, powerplant of the NASCAR stock car Short Track champion, this short-stroke V8 is capable of turning well over 5000 r.p.m. The Corvette makes it available in two versions: 210 h.p. with the single four-barrel carburetor, and 225 h.p. with dual four-barrel carburetors. A special high-performance cam is optional at extra cost.

For the driver who requires a superlative touring car rather than a competition machine the Corvette is available with such extra-cost lux-uries as removable hardtop, power-operated cloth top and window lifters, plus the Powerglide automatic transmission. And, for either choice, there is the assurance of reasonably priced service and parts at any of nearly 7500 Chevrolet dealerships.

If you are considering a sports car, don't fail to sample the 1956 Corvette. It is the surprise car of the year, as your Chevrolet dealer will be delighted to demonstrate.

CHEVROLET

CORVETTE

Instructions: Clip along the dotted line

After that, you're on your own.

But you'll think of something. That's a Corvette Sting Ray—Convertible on the left, Sport Coupe on the right. The name Corvette put America back on the sports car map and Corvette owners in a class by themselves.

Corvette did it, and does it, with a bon vivant of an extra-cost V8 that hits 375 hp, a ride you don't expect from sports cars, extravagant concern for your personal comfort, looks most stylists would be too timid to even suggest, and an elaborate style of doing things you probably thought went out with the last Roman emperor.

All this soul-soothing adventure without ever leaving civilization! A good dose of Corvette could forever change your mind about sports cars—and your Chevrolet dealer will lend a helping hand.

Chevrolet Division of General Motors, Detroit, Michigan.

'64 CORVETTE STING RAY BY CHEVROLET

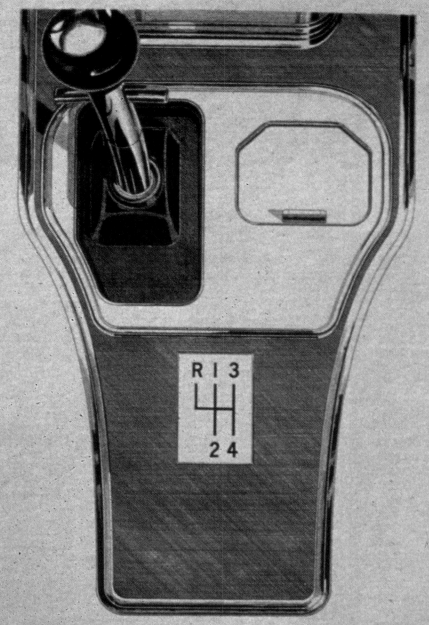

Flight 427, now departing through gates 1, 2, 3 and 4.

Pardon the word play, but Flight 427 is our way of informing you that Corvette can now be ordered with a 427-cubic-inch Turbo-Jet V8. We threw in the bit about the gates just to let you know our fully synchronized 4-speed's a must with this rig.

The regular-version 427 dispenses 390 hp and 460 lbs-ft of torque on hydraulic lifters, while the special-cam edition turns out 425 hp and the same amount of torque on solid lifters. Which one you order depends on whether you spend your time on the observation deck or the flight line.

Otherwise, we recommend our trusty 327 cubic-incher, available at ratings of either 300 or 350 horsepower. More than enough to slip the surly bonds with, eh, Orville?

You'd better believe it.

Corvette Performance The Chevrolet Way

'66 Corvette. Fasten your seat belts. They're standard.

Fair warning: Something about this one will get you all unglued. Maybe the slippery shape. Or maybe all that energy under the hood. Or the road-ready combination of independent suspension and disc brakes at all four corners. Whatever it is, the '68 Vette has got to be one of the most desirable cars ever built. So desirable, in fact, that you can order an exclusive new anti-theft warning system for it. Now, if anyone opens a door or the hood, he triggers a blurting, blaring horn. You might call it a piece of resistance for a pièce de résistance.

Corvette CHEVROLET

Perpetual emotion machine.

GM
MARK OF EXCELLENCE

A WORLD-CLASS CHAMPION PROVES IT YET AGAIN.

24 HOURS OF NELSON LEDGES

This was the race where some racing pundits claimed Corvette's dominance in showroom stock racing was supposed to have ended. The reason? The introduction of the Porsche 944 Turbo into SCCA showroom stock competition. Funny thing though. A lone '86 Corvette prototype beat the 944 Turbos by four laps in an event where none of the top three finishers suffered any major mechanical problems during the 24-hour race. Congratulations to the Morrison-Cook team and drivers Jim Cook, Don Knowles, Ron Grable and John Heinricy.

Despite increasing competition, the Nelson Ledges victory kept Corvette's unbeaten record intact in SCCA showroom stock enduro racing this season. But when you're a world-class champion, you don't mind proving it...again and again. **Chevy Thunder. The Heartbeat of America.**

ECHOES OF THUNDER... AT MONTEREY '87

CHEVROLET IS THE HONORED MARQUE AT THE '87 MONTEREY HISTORIC RACES.

Memories fade, but the machines live on.
They have lain quiet now, testimony to an era, stowed lovingly in dark garages and museums.

But on August 22-23, in Monterey, California, the tarps will come off. Fresh fuel will splash into their tanks. Starters will crank and those faded memories will explode to life with the most memorable sound in motorsports — Chevy thunder. Imagine a blue Corvette SS at Sebring, a bright orange McLaren at Elkhart Lake, a dark blue Corvette Gran Sport at the Bahamas, a white-winged Chaparral at LeMans.

Come to the Monterey Historic Races on August 22-23 and see the great thundering Chevrolets that re-wrote the history books and inspired generations of car enthusiasts. You'll also help Chevrolet salute 75 years of high performance.

The Corvette SS circa 1957
with its designer,
Zora Arkus Duntov,
behind the wheel.

Each year the Concours d'Elegance at California's distinguished Del Monte Lodge is a magnet for the world's handsomest sports cars. And in this fabulous setting, as on the road circuits, Corvette wears America's colors with honor.

WHEREVER THE WORLD'S BEST SPORTS CARS GATHER

CORVETTE DOES AMERICA PROUD!

by Chevrolet

From Pebble Beach to Paris one American car is accepted without question—Corvette. Because Corvette fulfills three necessary specifications superbly: It is an authentic sports car with competition-bred performance, supple suspension and startling roadability. It has beautifully polished road manners—a sweet and precise way of going, an inherent sense of direction and stability, a micrometric crispness of control. And it is utterly distinctive in line, shape and appointments, a subtly sculptured expression of function that is a constant fresh delight to the eye.

This is one of the truly great cars produced in all of America's motoring history. That is a proud achievement and we would like to share it with you. We suggest you see your Chevrolet dealer soon. Chevrolet Division of General Motors, Detroit 2, Michigan.

for ten seconds
try to imagine
what owning a
Corvette
would be like . . .

you're close,
but it's <u>better</u>
than that!

SOME GUYS HAVE IT
TOUGH

Corvette owners are not necessarily the most carefree people in the world, but there are moments when every Corvette driver must think himself thrice blest. Here's a car that, more than any other, has an uncanny ability to erase the day's cares and woes and whisk its driver far, far away. Turn on the key, engage first gear and step on it: Good-bye office, hello better things of life. We'll make no attempt to analyze the chemistry of such a phenomenon; it's all blurred by things like the feeling of wind on your face, the sound of the Corvette exhaust, the cyclone surge of a truly great V8 engine. We will be more than happy, however, to direct you to your nearest Chevrolet dealer to sample a Corvette. Look at it, sit in it, drive it, and you'll find that we haven't exaggerated a bit. We couldn't exaggerate these things if we tried. (Radio, as shown, optional at extra cost.) . . . Chevrolet Division of General Motors, Detroit 2, Michigan.

CORVETTE BY CHEVROLET

PAGES 201–216 Where drivers aspired to Corvettes, advertising copywriters hungered for the Corvette account, several making their name thanks to Chevrolet's finest, although the company itself never felt the need for all-out campaigns to sell the car. Most years the Corvette sold itself, as these advertisements show.

A Work of Art
(for your wall or garage).

(Scaled-down reproduction) of actual poster.

If ever a car deserved awe and respect, Corvette does. It's America's only true production sports car. And since its introduction in 1953, it has attained a level of recognition that is nearly legendary.

It's fitting, then, that Chevrolet is now honoring this remarkable automobile with an artful commemorative poster. The Corvette spirit is captured by one of the most respected automotive illustrators around, Ken Dallison.

Shown below is a section from this full-color, 36" by 31", suitable-for-framing poster. You'll discover important footnotes on the history and evolution of Corvette. Its design. Its features. Its recent pace car edition. And more.

You get it all for only $5.95 (including postage and handling). A small price to pay to put a legend on your wall. Don't you think?

Chevrolet

Ken Dallison

**LIMITED OFFER!
SEND FOR YOUR
FULL-COLOR
CORVETTE POSTER.**

ONLY **$5.95**

THE *Heartbeat* OF AMERICA IS RACING
CHEVROLET

A CAR SO UNBEATABLE THEY HAD TO CREATE ITS OWN RACE SERIES: THE CORVETTE CHALLENGE.

IT TAKES ONE TO BEAT ONE.

In the three years Corvette dominated the SS class of the SCCA Showroom Stock Endurance Championship, its record was 19-0. In fact, in 1987 Chevy won the Manufacturer's title by a modest 81-to-7 margin.

While we would be content to thrash our competition eternally, the gruesome sight proved to be too brutal for the SCCA. They mercifully called off the massacre.

So what do you do with a car in a class by itself?

You create a new class.

In the spirit of the International Race of Champions, SCCA sanctioned The Corvette Challenge Race Series.

Identical showroom stock 'Vettes (specially modified for racing) go head-to-head on the road and on the track. Ten races coast-to-coast. Up to 50 drivers competing for the richest showroom stock purse in SCCA history. A million dollars.

Corvette is the perfect example of how we use racing to develop, prove and improve the quality of the Chevys you'll buy tomorrow. We race to learn. Because at Chevrolet, quality is not just a word, it's a way of life.

The Corvette Challenge.

We already know what the best car is.

Now the challenge is to find out who the best driver is.

BEWARE THE RED BOWTIE.

Sponsored by Goodyear and Mid-America Design.
Produced by Powell Development America, Inc.

PIONEERS
OF
PERFECTION

A TECHNICAL HISTORY

THE Corvette has had more words written about it than any other Chevrolet and possibly more than all the others put together. That's because the Corvette is like no other Chevrolet; it has always been a pioneer. In many respects it was, and remained, crude, but in others it was years ahead of its time, so far out of the mainstream of GM products that its lead was never followed by the mass of Chevy sedans. It is almost as though the Corvette was built by an independent company — but then Duntov and his crew always strove to be a law unto themselves.

The first innovation of all was, of course, using fiberglass for the body. The Corvette wasn't the first 'glass car by any means, but certainly no one on the scale of GM had considered using such a material for a production car. It wasn't even as though Chevrolet were following the lead of some foreign manufacturers; of those companies that became famous for producing fiberglass-bodied cars (the likes of Lotus, TVR and Reliant in Britain and Matra in France) none even existed when plans for the Corvette were being drawn up. Lotus and Reliant both started in 1952, TVR a couple of years later and Matra did not appear until the mid '60s.

It was, however, the same forces that motivated these small embryonic British companies to use glassfibre (as it was termed over there) that motivated Chevrolet. There were three ways in which small-scale production could be satisfied and producing the proper, extremely expensive, dies for steel-body construction was not one of them. A method involving what are called Kirksite dies could have been employed to produce steel bodies at an economic rate, the dies having only a limited life and good for fewer than 10 000 units. That's very limited production in Chevrolet terms of course but, as it transpired, far more than early Corvette production figures.

Another method is to use aluminum, the approach of traditionalists like Aston Martin. That soft malleable metal can be easily worked and formed to beautiful shapes. . . as long as you have time and skilled craftsmen and expect to sell the car for a great deal of money. That approach was clearly out of the question to begin with and it had to be fiberglass or nothing. Aluminum was considered later for a unitary-bodied '58, but that came to naught.

Body-on-frame construction reigned supreme in 1950s America and the bodies were essentially clothing for the chassis rather than the main structural part of the car as is now the case, and the fiberglass was not expected to do more than substitute for those steel panels; the idea of producing a unitary-construction model did not even cross the designers' minds. Nevertheless, it was quickly realised that the only way to give the fiberglass sufficient rigidity was to make the body as near complete as possible, in the same way as an eggshell is remarkably tough despite being made of such fragile material. Consequently, the floor was molded as one complete component, sufficiently rigid (and light) for one man to hold it above his head, and one-handed at that, as a famous GM publicity picture proved.

The top was made in two main sections, the first stretching back to the end of the doors and the second consisting of the rear fenders and apron. When they were bonded to the floor and attached to the frame, the resulting structure was very rigid indeed, so much so that one of the prototypes which rolled over at GM's proving ground survived remarkably intact, as did its driver.

Altogether the body was made up of just nine sections — very few indeed when you consider that certain panels (hood, trunk, doors) by their very nature have to be separate. It was a very successful construction, helped by the fact that, being only a two-seater, the cockpit opening was small and the shell thus stiff enough for the original 0.2in thick fiberglass to be thinned down to the 0.1in section used in production. That

improvement also owed a lot to research on the material (novel to GM) which showed how the process itself could be refined. The original bodies were by no means masterpieces, but they showed that it could be done.

That was a matter of supreme indifference to Chevrolet as a whole, GM and the rest of the US auto industry; when Ford produced their 'Corvette' in the shape of the T-bird, it was in steel and remained so. Fiberglass was totally unrealistic for volume construction, being extremely labor-intensive, and there was very little incentive for Corvette engineers to try to maximise the use of 'glass. It had not been chosen to exploit one of its main characteristics, its light weight; the Corvette's size alone would ensure that it was light in relation to the off-the-shelf production engines it would inevitably have to use. It was the production reality of having to use existing (and heavy) sedan running gear that precluded such interesting experiments in fiberglass construction as the first Lotus Elite or the intriguing (if very obscure) Rochdale Olympic, two British designs that did away with the frame altogether, making the fiberglass body into a true monocoque, the Olympic with a one-piece moulding, the Lotus with six main body sections bonded together. Metal load-bearing reinforcements were bonded in at appropriate places, but neither car was a success and Corvette engineers wisely held off until the 1980s and the creation of the latest-generation Vettes before doing anything in the least innovative with the plastic body.

As for the chassis, that of the first Corvette followed standard procedure in being an X-braced perimeter frame swept up at the rear to clear the live axle hung on the usual system of semi-elliptic leaf springs which were mounted outboard of the main chassis rails giving better axle location, an innovation that was taken up by Chevrolet sedans. Front suspension was essentially the A-arm system used on the 1949–54 Chevrolets although, to take into account the Vette's lighter weight and intended different ride characteristics, spring and shock rates were modified accordingly. Steering was nothing out of the ordinary either, being Saginaw's recirculating-ball system with its ratio quickened to 16:1.

It all served its purpose, and continued to do so basically little changed in concept for many years. It was simple and easy to set up, the initial design needing only a slight tweak from Duntov to produce a neutral-handling stance, a tweak consisting of adding two degrees of positive caster at the front and slightly relocating the rear spring mounts.

Duntov being a purist at heart, albeit a practical one, had always hankered after independent rear suspension; he couldn't see how a proper sports car could get by without it. It was true that those British traditionalists the Triumph TR3/4 and the MGA and MGB got by with live rear axles but Duntov was after bigger fish. The Mercedes 300SL provided race-track competition for the Corvette in the '50s and it had a most involved, although (to modern eyes) fundamentally unsound swing-axle rear suspension, while every Porsche built had an independent system, too, albeit one equally flawed. But when the Jaguar XK-E (E-type) burst on the scene in 1961, it was clear that independent rear suspension (irs) was at last being done properly in a sports car and the Corvette finally jumped on the bandwagon.

Duntov had done his best with the live axle; the '59 car, for example, had more emphasis placed on the anti-sway bars rather than stiff springs in an attempt to get the best of both worlds, compliance in the suspension when both front or rear wheels hit a bump but lateral stiffness to help its cornering poise. That was only an interim measure and irs appeared on the third-generation Corvette in 1963.

The range of existing irs systems was extensive, but none fitted the bill for Duntov. The usual explanation for the strange design he came up with was that there was insufficient room to allow conventional, upright, coil springs but it's hard to give that too much credence as the rival XK-E was shallower in the rear deck *and* had a narrower track and yet no fewer than four coil springs were accommodated in its sophisticated rear-suspension system.

Duntov, however, opted for a cheaper system involving a transverse multi-leaf spring mounted below the differential on a curved longitudinal chassis member which, together with a transverse member, formed a T-shaped subframe, rubber bushed to insulate driveline vibration from the main chassis. The driveshafts were articulated at each end (rather than at one end only in the superficially similar system used on the contemporary Triumph Spitfire) to form the upper arms of a 'double-wishbone' arrangement. That was exactly the same as in the XK-E. In the Corvette, the lower transverse spring was relieved of much of its locating duties by the presence of a transverse radius rod each side running from the diff-carrier subframe sideways and slightly forwards to a lower mounting bracket on the hub carrier, which was also the lower mount for the telescopic shocks. The main fore and aft location, however, was via a substantial, if short, trailing arm per side.

It was by no means as 'pure' as the XK-E suspension but crucially its manufacturing costs were low. As far as Chevrolet were concerned, independent rear suspension was an indulgence and one that would only be granted if it could be fitted into the budget. Duntov accordingly made economies by using Chevrolet sedan components in the double A-arm front suspension, which worked just fine after a hydraulic steering damper eliminated the front's sensitivity to wheel alignment.

A curious-looking design the irs may have been but it satisfied the main criteria of providing accurate wheel location and reducing unsprung weight. What other GM car at the time had an independent rear end in 1963? Strangely enough, the Corvette didn't stand completely alone in this respect: Chevrolet's disastrous venture into rear-engined design in the shape of the Corvair had irs but that was inescapable given the location of the engine, while another of GM's divisions had produced an equally disastrous car with an independent rear. Prompted by a certain John Z. De Lorean, Pontiac had produced the Tempest sedan with a swing-axle system that was even more horrible than most such designs and that may well have had something to do with Chevrolet's luke-warm attitude. But Duntov's persistance paid off and the Corvette pioneered the first successful independent rear end.

In other respects, the Corvette broke new ground before the advent of irs, pioneering fuel injection, for example. In the fifties, Mercedes-Benz were about the only company taking injection seriously; a Bosch system featured on the 300SL, for example, helping its 2996cc straight-six produce 215bhp at 6200rpm. The Ramjet continuous-flow mechanical injection system used on the Corvette was made by GM's Rochester Carburetor Division, although Duntov and Cadillac's Harry Barr played quite a part in refining it and getting it properly sorted. When you consider that it's only recently that GM was trumpeting the claims of the crude throttle-body, single-point 'Crossfire' injection (a sort of halfway house between injection and carburetor), the Ramjet seems very advanced for the '50s, with individual port injection and the fuel metered according to air flow.

To keep the record straight, however, it should be noted that the injection system was not built for the Corvette alone: it was also intended for higher-volume sedan use, and a special version of the 283cu in V8 was built for the Ramjet, with heavy-duty bearings, an improved ignition system and solid rather than the customary hydraulic lifters.

It was a brave attempt, but injection failed on several counts. It did enable the 283 to produce 283bhp, but that was only a fraction more than the twin four-barrel carb set-up could crank out far more cheaply and, until the injectors were lengthened to protrude more into a cooling airstream, rough idling (extremely uncharacteristic of injection) resulted. The flat spot it suffered during early development was also the very opposite of what you hope to achieve with injection. It did give performance, though — 'fuelies' could knock off 0–60 times of just over six seconds.

Nevertheless, injection proved a dead end in the '50s: it wasn't as reliable as the uncomplicated downdraft carb and it was expensive. When GM finally killed it off in 1965, it was a $500 option and that was a substantial premium over twenty years ago, particularly as you could get almost as much power from a four-barrel Holley.

There were other aspects where the Corvette was given developments out of the Chevrolet mainstream. Aluminum may not have made it for the body on the '58, but the Corvette certainly made more use of the material than anyone else at the time. In 1960, the Corvette was given an alloy radiator which gave a weight saving of fifty per cent, and the alloy clutch housing which followed was an even more worthwhile reducer of weight. Set alongside the weight of a cast-iron V8, of course, having an alloy clutch housing was only scraping the surface and that prompted the development of alloy cylinder heads in 1960 in high-silicon aluminum. Unfortunately, the experiment was not a success, Chevrolet finding, like other manufacturers before and since, that alloy would warp whereas heavier cast iron was totally trouble-free.

More successful was using aluminum for the casing of the four-speed manual transmission also offered in 1960. The (mostly) successful experiments with aluminum prompted the Corvette team to use it to cure the car's notorious brake-fade problem. Large, 11in diameter, finned alloy brake drums were introduced in '63 and they, of course, dissipated heat far better than the standard cast-iron drums and saved on unsprung weight into the bargain, as did the alloy wheels the Corvette offered long before the opposition.

Alloy brake drums were a solution of sorts, but a very old-fashioned one reminiscent of the die-hard approach of Ferrari in Formula One. Ferrari shunned the far more effective disc brakes for years, as their enormous elegant finned drums bore testimony, while in the Corvette's case it was economic reality rather than pure stubbornness that forced the alloy drums — all through the Corvette's life there has been this tension between cost-cutting and innovation that has forced development into some interesting areas. Despite experiments with other powerplants from time to time, the Corvette was always destined to be motivated by a V8 — nothing else made economic sense and nothing else could give such power for the price. The steadily increasing use of alloy castings was the most sensible way of compensating for the weight of the V8 in a small car. The brakes, in contrast, just showed that the Corvette didn't warrant the discs that the XK-E was flaunting to such good effect in 1961.

The Corvette did get its discs in due course, but it wasn't until the '65 model year that Delco could come up with a suitable system: one that featured two-part, four-pot calipers operating on vented rotors, and one which provided the necessary dramatically improved braking.

Despite all the clever weight-paring that went on, the Corvette had grown to be a very heavy two-seater indeed by the late 1970s, as the long unchanging generation introduced in '68 wore on. It was a combination of the iron V8, the heavy ladder chassis with its five cross-members (introduced back in '63) and the hardly spartan interior. By the end of its life in '82, the fourth-generation Corvette weighed in excess of 3400lb. That seemed to make a mockery of all the clever use of alloy components and the more recent (1981) development of a plastic monofilament leaf spring that tipped the scales at a mere 7lb rather than the 33lb of the standard multi-leaf steel assembly. Not to mention the fiberglass body. . . .

A total redesign was called for and yet two of the car's most old-fashioned features were retained for the next generation: the 350cu in V8 and the front-engine, rear-drive configuration. The engine was never seriously in doubt, for the Corvette had to be at the top of the domestic heap, clearly above such potentially exciting new models as the Pontiac Fiero and in no danger of looking less muscular than Pontiac's Trans-Am or Chevrolet's own Z28 Camaro. So the 350 it was, and it soon became clear that the best place for it was the traditional location under the hood at the front of the car. It seemed an odd decision when the new Vette was supposed to be more than able to hold its own with the best of the world's exotic cars, yet still offer reasonable cabin space and trunk capacity, something which would have been a monumental task using the V8 in either a transverse or longitudinal mid-engined design. That was the explanation given by head of Corvette engineering Dave McLellan (Duntov's successor, appointed in 1975) and, in fact, you could argue that he took the braver decision in sticking with the front-engined, rear-drive format, risking ridicule in the specialist press.

The mid-engined Aerovette concept car of 1977 looked favorite as the basis of the new Corvette until McLellan stepped back, took an objective look at the conventional layout and realised that, properly executed, it could give everything that was required. The engine could be mounted back far enough to give an even weight distribution; it wouldn't have the same low polar moment of inertia as a mid-engined design, but its weight was still well within the wheelbase, avoiding the 'dumb-bell' effect of designs such as the 944 Porsche with its engine at one end and transaxle the other.

Once that was established, the vital considerations were suspension design and calibration, and that was given the utmost attention. A car's only point of contact with the road is through its tires and McLellan's design worked back from the tire. To him, maximizing the potential of the best tire available was the essence of good suspension design if your criteria are performance and handling rather than ride. Modern low-profile tires are designed to work (*have* to work) with all their tread on the road so camber changes have to be kept to an absolute minimum, as does roll because the way to maximize the tires' grip is to have all four contributing as long as possible. The solution could only be double unequal-length wishbones at the front, following previous practice, an intriguing new design at the rear and some astonishingly high spring rates, almost race-car hard. At the back, a single transverse link per side connecting hub carrier to diff carrier gave the longest, and the purest, movement with none of the subtle shifts in suspension geometry that even the best semi-trailing-arm systems suffer. The double-jointed driveshafts once again acted as upper links with the composite transverse rear spring having little part to play in

locating the wheels. Fore and aft movements and torque reactions were controlled by four trailing rods and a single rear tie rod per side, while the final element was an anti-sway bar.

Aiming for the biggest wheel and tire package possible has a weight penalty, ameliorated in the Corvette's case by more extensive use of weight-saving materials in the suspension than any other production car made. The front wishbones were alloy forgings, as were the rear transverse links, and the brake calipers (which had to be huge to deal with the Corvette's performance) were cast from an iron-aluminum alloy. Driveshafts were forged alloy and the springs were of extremely resilient and light composite material. The 'plastic' monofilament rear leaf spring which debuted in '81 had been such a success it was duplicated for the front suspension where it ran under the engine and worked on the lower wishbones.

The design team had a ball trying to find components that could be made lighter. The old heavy steel ladder frame was junked and front and back of the car joined together by a single C-shaped beam running from the alloy transmission housing to the alloy diff housing. It would be stretching a point somewhat to call it a chassis, although the front suspension and the engine were effectively held in a conventional perimeter frame, the front legs of which extended forward to the bumper area to take frontal impacts. For the new Corvette, the design team had come up with an interesting structure — not quite body-on-frame but not quite unitary or monocoque either. Chevrolet, too, were obviously not sure how to describe it, giving it the rather peculiar tag 'integral perimeter-birdcage unitized structure'. If you see the car on the assembly line, however, you can see what they mean. A very deep transmission-tunnel section combined with floor and bulkheads to form a stiff passenger shell, of light high-strength steel completed at the top by steel windscreen supports (for the most steeply raked 'screen ever seen on a US production car) which ideally would have been continued back along the roof to join up with the B-pillar posts which were joined to form a roll-over hoop. Joining front and rear wasn't practical, though, as a full convertible was always intended and it was felt vital that the coupe be as airy as possible. This entailed a lift-out roof panel which would have looked bizarre with front and rear posts joined together. Clearly, the main strength lay in the center tub which also provided the pick-up points for the rear-suspension trailing arms.

The body itself continued to be made of fiberglass and although, as in any 'glass car, it adds to the strength and stiffness of the whole structure once it's in place, it still wasn't intended to be a major contributor to the chassis. In fact, it is actually slightly misleading to call the current generation of Corvettes fiberglass. The Fiero had shown just how impressive SMC (sheet molding compound) plastic could be used for body panels, and the same material was used on the '84 Corvette for its enormous hood and for other far more minor details such as the radiator brackets. SMC is amazingly tough and resilient and ideally suited to the Fiero application where it was used merely as cladding; the Corvette's body, in contrast, is far more of a separate structure and one more suited to the more rigid fiberglass.

SMC, fiberglass, plastic-composite springs, cast-alloy driveshafts and suspension arms — all most impressive. However, the '84 Corvette, not radically different in size from its predecessor, still tipped the scales at over 3200lb, only a couple of hundred pounds lighter than its archaic forebear. Part of the explanation lay in the very high level of equipment needed to make the car a match for its exotic and luxurious rivals.

It's too easy to criticize; sure the car was heavy, but it was never intended to be an economy car and a glance at the specifications of its rivals show it in a better light. Take the Porsche 928, for example (as McLellan's team did during development). It, too, is a front-engined V8 with surprisingly similar dimensions and yet, even though the Porsche flagship can boast a sophisticated overhead-cam all-alloy V8, the 928 is actually *heavier* than the Corvette, and no other Vette rival pretends to be a real lightweight, either.

Lotus used to build down to the lightest weight possible but even their latest supercar, the recently revised Esprit Turbo, breaks the 3000lb barrier. Overall, the Corvette team succeeded in their aim of maximising the potential of the front-engined rear-drive system, not with the '84 on its ludicrously stiff suspension settings but certainly with the later models, and the latest, the ZR1, proves the point: 0–60 in just over 4 secs, 12-second quarter-miles and a top speed approaching 175mph in a chassis that makes it usable.

One of a number of intriguing features on the ZR1 is its *six*-speed manual transmission, which is in marked contrast to the Corvette's very first gearbox, the Powerglide two-speed auto. Despite the massive torque of the V8s that have powered the Vette for virtually all its life, Corvette engineers only briefly gave into the temptation to rely on the traditional three-speed auto, producing alloy-cased, four-speed manuals and then, for the '84, one of the most bizarre overdrives ever devised (and one of the least successful). It operated on the top three ratios and automatically engaged itself until the driver pressed hard on the throttle, whereupon the transmission kicked-down just like an automatic. It was far less satisfying than the old Laycock system used on ancient British roadsters (and current Volvos) where a switch activated the higher ratio when the driver decided. With the change quality itself being heavy and generally dreadful, it wasn't one of the car's most successful features and it was there only to give the manual Vette fuel economy inside the Federal-regulation limits before incurring the politically unacceptable (for Chevrolet) gas-guzzler tax.

Development on the current-generation cars has solved the transmission problem; Corvette Engineering and the German gearbox manufacturers ZF collaborated to produce the ML9 six-speed which still boasts overdriven upper ratios and computer-aided gear selection (CAGS) that will shift you from first to fourth if you're merely loafing; when you mean business it reverts to a normal manual transmission. The transmission is in gas-saving mode only when the engine is warm, speed between 12 and 19mph and the throttle less than thirty-five per cent open. Those criteria are met often enough for a fuel saving to be made.

Transmissions are designed to make the best of the engine and the Corvette has had some mighty powerplants in its time. Although the story of Vette engines is really that of the American V8, there have been some innovative and interesting motors under those fiberglass hoods and the first one of all was one of the more noteworthy. . . and it was only a six.

The 235cu in (3.8-liter) straight-six, the 'Stovebolt Six' was in fact a light-truck engine adapted for sedan use with the advent of the Powerglide transmission; the standard 216cu in was a pre-war design that simply lacked sufficient power and torque. Not that the Stovebolt was dramatically more powerful; to equip it for sedan use its output was increased to the dizzy heights of 105bhp (gross, of course) at 3600rpm.

That was all Duntov had to work with, yet he was able significantly to increase its power, to 150bhp at a higher engine speed of 4200rpm.

The cam was changed to give higher valve-lift and longer valve-opening, the head was skimmed to raise compression ratio from 7.5:1 to 8.0:1 and its breathing was improved by incorporating three Carter YH sidedraft carbs on an alloy intake manifold (one carb for two cylinders) and a freer-flowing exhaust system. The engine was tidied up, renamed the Blue Flame, made slightly more compact with a new rocker cover, its water cooling system upgraded and there it was, a respectable powerplant, made more respectable when another new cam give it a further 5bhp. That was enough to give 11-second 0–60 times and a top speed of 106mph.

Then came the V8, the immortal Chevy small block. It was the work of Ed Cole who was so confident of his design that it went straight from the drawing board to production tooling. That wasn't very surprising as Cole knew V8s inside and out, had been Cadillac's chief engineer since 1936 and had designed Cadillac's post-war V8. He had long had a vision of the 'ideal' V8 that he would build given the opportunity; it would have a displacement of 26cu in (4.3 liters) and, given Cole's established ideas of ideal cylinder size and the desirability of oversquare dimensions, the bore and stroke virtually chose themselves at 3.75in × 3.0in. With such a displacement, there was no need for a long stroke to generate torque (as in the old six) and the V8's 260lb ft at 3000rpm was a perfect complement to the 195bhp at 5000rpm the V8 produced in Corvette trim (some thirty-three per cent more than in the sedan), a figure that grew to 225bhp in '56 thanks to a 9.25:1 compression ratio and the 'Duntov cam' which opened the valves longer (although no higher) and allowed an engine speed of 6500rpm in high-performance trim.

The concept was exactly right and the virtues of the V8 had long been realised: it's compact with a short crank that can be perfectly supported on five main bearings and V8s can be made respectably light for the number of cylinders, even using cast iron. In fact, the 265 was as much as 40lb lighter than the old Blue Flame Six. Cole's engine was simple and yet clever, with features such as individual rocket pivots with the valve-gap adjustment in the rocker pivot rather than on the rocker itself, the system used when there's a common rocker shaft. The arrangement saved on reciprocating weight and materials, as did the use of hollow pushrods to circulate the oil to the valvegear.

The scope of the small-block V8 was enormous, for it had the potential for enlarging both the bore and the stroke. First the bore grew to 3.875in to produce the 283cu in and then in 1962 both bore and stroke were increased to 4.0in and 3.25in respectively to form the 327 which, in its L76 and L84 guises in 1964, produced impressive quantities of pure power. The L76 with a single four-barrel carb and a compression ratio that had risen all the way from the 7.5:1 of the original V8 nearly 10 years before to the dizzy heights of 11.25:1 had a massive output of 365bhp at 6200rpm — so much for the image of the V8 as just a crude low-revving device. The L84 differed in having fuel injection and that boosted output further, to 375bhp at the same engine speed.

That was surely enough power for anyone but, much like the arms race, the horsepower race between Ford, GM and Chrysler got out of hand: the result for the Corvette was the advent of the big-block V8 in 1966. That engine design had been around since 1963 when it appeared for the Daytona 500. It differed from the small block not only in size, the two versions displacing 396cu in and 427cu in (6.5 and 7 liters), but in the odd valvegear arrangement developed by designer Robert Benzinger. Naturally, it was still a pushrod overhead-valve system, but the decision to angle the valves to produce a more efficient combustion chamber dictated that the pushrods be set at odd angles, giving rise to its Porcupine nickname.

The inlet valves were angled 26 degrees from the cylinder axis and the exhausts at 17 degrees. Viewed from the side, the valves were also angled, one forward and one back, by 9 degrees, from the angle at which the pushrods operated so there was no wasted sideways movement between rods and rocker arms. In other respects, it was standard V8, although beefed up compared with the small block to deal with the high torque and power. The main bearings were a substantial 2.75in in diameter and width was increased, too.

Both the 396 and 427 were kept oversquare with dimensions of 4.1 × 3.76in and 4.25 × 3.75in, respectively, and even the 427 could rev more than respectably, the best of the bunch being the L72 with 11.0:1 compression ratio and a staggering 425bhp at 6400rpm from its four-barrel Holley and solid lifters. Torque was 'only' 396lb ft, indicating that the L72 was indeed a tuned engine, enough to drive 0—60 times down to nearer 5 seconds than 6, with staggering standing-quarter-mile times below 13 secs at a terminal speed over 110mph. You don't need twelve cylinders, quad cams and more valves than you can keep track of to produce the goods!

It worked, but it wasn't the ideal for someone like Duntov; more like it was the stunning L88 with its alloy cylinder heads, extraordinary compression ratio of 12.5:1, race cam and enormous Holley four-barrel rated at 850 cubic feet per minute. It was based on the 427, but in reality it was a peaky race engine out of place in any road car, even a Corvette. Chevrolet rated it at 435bhp, but that was a deliberate political understatement and, in fact, its true output was certainly over 500bhp, some experts putting it as high as 560; for all that power, it weighed only 60lb or so more than the small block, however.

Even the L88 wasn't the ultimate, though; that

has to be the ZL-1, an all-alloy version of the 427 which was an unashamed development of Bruce McLaren's Can-Am engine. Its alloy block made it even lighter than the L88 while its conservative power rating was even further from the truth than the L88's claim. With only 116 L88s built, along with a mere two ZL-1s, such power wasn't typical of the Vette but even the mainstream cars of the period boasted 350bhp.

It wasn't all V8s, however, for there was the unhappy episode of the Wankel rotary, although in some ways that was peripheral to the Corvette. Ed Cole went on to become GM President but his interest in engines never waned. He secured the production rights to the Wankel for $50 million and there were plans to launch it first in the Vega and then in new small front-drive sedans. At one stage, between 165 000 and 200 000 Vegas were planned for the '75 model year. But, to no one's surprise, the rotary could not meet the increasingly stringent emissions regulations while maintaining anything like reasonable fuel economy.

The Wankel's main attraction for the Corvette was simply one of packaging. Duntov had been pushing the XP-882 styling exercise towards production. That was a mid-engined concept designed to take as many stock parts from the front-drive Olds Tornado as possible (following the normal Corvette route of maximising the use of existing components). The big V8 was mounted transversely behind the driver with chain drive to the gearbox mounted below the front bank of cylinders. What with this and convoluted packaging problems, involving drive shafts running through sumps, John De Lorean was right to cancel the project. The Wankel allowed the mid-engined concept to be revived, to the extent that of two Wankel-engined cars made (one a two-rotor model designed by Pininfarina, the other Bill Mitchell's 420bhp four-rotor), the Mitchell car

survived the demise of the Wankel to be re-equipped with a small-block V8 and renamed the Aerovette. That was essentially Dave McLellan's starting point for the fifth-generation cars, a point he soon moved away from as cars like the Porsche 928 showed what could be done with a front-mounted V8. The De Lorean had shown that gull-wing doors were still a problem and elements like the V-shaped front screen really didn't seem terribly practical. McLellan's solution, in contrast, was almost ideal, a rare combination of the sensible and the exotic, a Corvette you could use on days when you would leave the Ferrari in the garage.

When the first of McLellan's cars, the '84, appeared, critics were impressed but they probably didn't understand quite how much potential it had, potential realised in the ZR1 option of the '89 model.

Continuing the engine theme, the original plan for the ZR1 was the incorporation of thirty-two valves for the current V8 (in other words, four per cylinder) and Lotus were approached for the job. Lotus chief engineer Tony Rudd, however, was persuasive enough to convince Chevrolet that what they really needed was a whole new engine. . . . It turned out to be a 350cu in, too, although with a smaller bore of 3.9in and consequently a longer stroke of 3.66in. Where it really differs from the standard engine is in its construction and valvegear.

Echoing the old L88 427 the LT5, as it's called, is all alloy, unusually even using alloy wet liners Nikasil plated. Even the oil pan is alloy but the engine's strength is guaranteed by iron main-bearing caps that extend into the lower crankcase. The cross-drilled crank is in forged steel, as are the connecting rods and the whole engine is balanced for smoothness and long life.

Although it's possible to operate four valves per cylinder with a single overhead cam, the accepted system is to use twin cams, one for the two inlets, one for the two exhausts, and that was the method used by Lotus with chain drive to the cams. The included valve angle was kept narrow, at 22 degrees, to make the engine compact enough to fit under an unchanged hood.

A four-valve design allows better breathing of course (the surface area of four small valves being greater than that of two larger ones) but the design allows the Corvette to adopt a particularly clever induction system which shows what can be done when engineers are forced to combine such incompatible objectives as high performance and fuel economy.

There's sequential fuel injection, of course, with an injector for each of the sixteen inlets, which also have their own individual air intake. The LT5 virtually has two induction systems, one for ordinary road performance (and good economy), using just one inlet valve per cylinder and the other using both for maximum power and performance. To achieve that, the intake ports, valves and cam lobes are divided into two groups, the primary towards the front of the engine, the secondary to the rear. The secondary ports are slightly larger in diameter and contain a port-throttle butterfly, the action of which is computer controlled.

In normal operation, the secondary-port throttle is closed so no air-fuel can pass through the second inlet valve. Past 3500rpm the throttle opens, the engine breathes freely and the power climbs dramatically and to satisfy its thirst the secondary valve is operated by a cam lobe with more duration than the primary, holding it open

longer. In 'power' mode the LT5 is nudging 400bhp and 400lb ft of torque.

Such an induction system isn't new — Toyota have something similar on their twin-cams, although without the variable valve timing — but it's none the less clever and *most* unusual on a V8. Also clever is the ignition system which uses direct coil ignition with four coils for the eight cylinders, each coil firing two cylinders with the coils triggered by a crankshaft sensor.

It's not just the engine that's smart; the ZR1 may not have the active ride that was once envisaged but it does have no fewer than eighteen shock absorber settings, divided into three modes: Touring, Sport and Competition, each mode being progressively stiffer. Within each mode the damper setting is made progressively harder as speed rises and, at high speed, whichever mode has been selected, the automatic override takes over and gives you the hardest setting for maximum handling (and safety).

The mechanics of the system (developed jointly with Bilstein) involve electrically powered actuators which rotate the valve according to the commands of the control module, acting on information from the speed sensors and mode position.

In a little over a quarter of a century the Corvette has come a long way indeed; the buyer of a two-speed Powerglide six in 1953 would be amazed by the ZR1 with its six-speed computer-controlled transmission and alloy quad-cam V8, but he would still recognize the Corvette as a classic sports car from a traditional mold, a synthesis any designer would be proud of.

CORVETTE ENGINES

Year	Type	Bore	Stroke	Displacement	Horsepower	rpm	Compression ratio	Fuel System	Option Code (RPO)
1953	OHV inline 6	3.560	3.96	235.5	150	4200	8.0:1	3 single-throats	Std
1954	inline 6	3.560	3.96	235.5	155	4200	8.0:1	3 single-throats	Std
1955	inline 6	3.560	3.96	235.5	155	4200	8.0:1	3 single-throats	2934–6
	OHV V8	3.750	3.00	265	195	5000	8.0:1	Dual four-barrel	2934–8
1956	V8	3.750	3.00	265	210	5200	9.25:1	Single four-barrel	Std
	V8	3.750	3.00	265	225	5200	9.25:1	Dual four-barrel	449
	V8	3.750	3.00	265	240	5800	9.25:1	Dual four-barrel	469
1957	V8	3.875	3.00	283	220	4800	9.5:1	Single four-barrel	Std
	V8	3.875	3.00	283	245	5000	9.5:1	Dual four-barrel	469A
	V8	3.875	3.00	283	250	5000	9.5:1	Fuel injection	579A
	V8	3.875	3.00	283	270	6000	9.5:1	Dual four-barrel	469B
	V8	3.875	3.00	283	283	6200	10.5:1	Fuel injection	579B
	V8	3.875	3.00	283	283	6200	10.5:1	Fuel injection	579E
1958	V8	3.875	3.00	283	230	4800	9.5:1	Single four-barrel	Std
	V8	3.875	3.00	283	245	5000	9.5:1	Dual four-barrel	469
	V8	3.875	3.00	283	250	5000	9.5:1	Fuel injection	579
	V8	3.875	3.00	283	270	6000	9.5:1	Dual four-barrel	469C
	V8	3.875	3.00	283	290	6200	10.5:1	Fuel injection	579D
1959	V8	3.875	3.00	283	230	4800	9.5:1	Single four-barrel	Std
	V8	3.875	3.00	283	245	5000	9.5:1	Dual four-barrel	469
	V8	3.875	3.00	283	250	5000	9.5:1	Fuel injection	579
	V8	3.875	3.00	283	270	6000	9.5:1	Duel four-barrel	469C
	V8	3.875	3.00	283	290	6200	10.5:1	Fuel injection	579D
1960	V8	3.875	3.00	283	230	4800	9.5:1	Single four-barrel	Std
	V8	3.875	3.00	283	245	5000	9.5:1	Dual four-barrel	469
	V8	3.875	3.00	283	270	6000	9.5:1	Dual four-barrel	469C
	V8	3.875	3.00	283	275	5200	11.0:1	Fuel injection	579
	V8	3.875	3.00	283	315	6200	11.0:1	Fuel injection	579D
1961	V8	3.875	3.00	283	230	4800	9.5:1	Single four-barrel	Std
	V8	3.875	3.00	283	245	5000	9.5:1	Dual four-barrel	469
	V8	3.875	3.00	283	270	6000	9.5:1	Dual four-barrel	468
	V8	3.875	3.00	283	275	5200	11.0:1	Fuel injection	353
	V8	3.875	3.00	283	315	6200	11.0:1	Fuel injection	354
1962	V8	4.000	3.25	327	250	4400	10.5:1	Simple four-barrel	Std
	V8	4.000	3.25	327	300	5000	10.5:1	Single four barrel	L75
	V8	4.000	3.25	327	340	6000	11.25:1	Single four-barrel	L76
	V8	4.000	3.25	327	360	6000	11.25:1	Fuel injection	582
1963	V8	4.000	3.25	327	250	4400	10.5:1	Single four-barrel	Std
	V8	4.000	3.25	327	300	5000	10.5	Single four-barrel	L75
	V8	4.000	3.25	327	340	6000	11.25	Single four-barrel	L76
	V8	4.000	3.25	327	360	6000	11.25	Fuel injection	L84
1964	V8	4.000	3.25	327	250	4400	10.5:1	Single four-barrel	Std
	V8	4.000	3.25	327	300	5000	10.5	Single four-barrel	L75
	V8	4.000	3.25	327	365	6200	11.25	Single four-barrel	L76
	V8	4.000	3.25	327	375	6200	11.25	Fuel injection	L84

CORVETTE ENGINES

Year	Type	Bore	Stroke	Displacement	Horsepower	rpm	Compression ratio	Fuel System	Option Code (RPO)
1965	V8	4.000	3.25	327	250	4400	10.5:1	Single four-barrel	Std
	V8	4.000	3.25	327	300	5000	10.5	Single four-barrel	L75
	V8	4.000	3.25	327	350	5800	11.25	Single four-barrel	L79
	V8	4.000	3.25	327	365	6200	11.25	Single four-barrel	L76
	V8	4.000	3.25	327	375	6200	11.25	Fuel injection	L84
	V8	4.090	3.76	396	425	6400	11.0:1	Single four-barrel	L78
1966	V8	4.000	3.25	327	300	5000	10.5:1	Single four-barrel	Std
	V8	4.000	3.25	327	350	5800	11.5:1	Single four-barrel	L79
	V8	4.250	3.75	427	390	5400	10.25:1	Single four-barrel	L36
	V8	4.250	3.75	427	425	6400	11.0:1	Single four-barrel	L72
1967	V8	4.000	3.25	327	300	5000	10.25:1	Single four-barrel	Std
	V8	4.000	3.25	327	350	5800	11.0:1	Single four-barrel	L79
	V8	4.250	3.75	427	390	5400	10.25:1	Single four-barrel	L36
	V8	4.250	3.75	427	400	5400	10.25:1	Single four-barrel	L68
	V8	4.250	3.75	427	435	5800	11.0:1	Tripower	L71
	V8	4.250	3.75	427	560	5800	12.5:1	Single four-barrel	L88
1968	V8	4.000	3.25	327	300	5000	10.5:1	Single four-barrel	Std
	V8	4.250	3.75	427	350	5800	11.0:1	Single four-barrel	L79
	V8	4.250	3.75	427	390	5400	10.25:1	Single four-barrel	L36
	V8	4.250	3.75	427	400	5400	10.25:1	Tripower	L68
	V8	4.250	3.75	427	435	5800	11.0:1	Tripower	L71
	V8	4.250	3.75	427	435	5800	11.0:1	Tripower	L89
	V8	4.250	3.75	427	560	5800	12.5:1	Single four-barrel	L88
1969	V8	4.000	3.48	350	300	4800	10.25:1	Single four-barrel	Std
	V8	4.000	3.48	350	350	5600	11.0:1	Single four-barrel	L46
	V8	4.250	3.75	427	390	5400	10.25:1	Single four-barrel	L36
	V8	4.250	3.75	427	400	5400	10.25:1	Tripower	L68
	V8	4.250	3.75	427	435	5800	11.0:1	Tripower	L71
	V8	4.250	3.75	427	435	5200	12.5:1	Tripower	L89
	V8	4.250	3.75	427	500			Single four-barrel	L88
	V8	4.250	3.75	427	500			Single four-barrel	ZL1
1970	V8	4.000	3.48	350	300	4800	10.25:1	Single four-barrel	Std
	V8	4.000	3.48	350	350	5600	11.0:1	Single four-barrel	L46
	V8	4.000	3.48	350	370	6000	11.0:1	Single four-barrel	LT1
	V8	4.250	4.00	454	390	4800	10.25:1	Single four-barrel	LS5
	V8	4.250	4.00	454	465	5200	12.25:1		N/A
1971	V8	4.000	3.48	350	270	4800	8.5:1	Single four-barrel	Std
	V8	4.000	3.48	350	330	5600	9.01	Single four-barrel	LT1
	V8	4.000	3.48	350	330			Single four-barrel	ZR1
	V8	4.250	4.00	454	365	4800	8.5:1	Single four-barrel	LS5
	V8	4.250	4.00	454	425	5600	9.0:1	Single four-barrel	LS6
	V8	4.250	4.00	454	425	5600	9.0:1	Single four-barrel	ZR2
1972	V8	4.000	3.48	350	200				LS4
	V8	4.000	3.48	350	255			Single four-barrel	LT1
	V8	4.000	3.48	350	255			Single four-barrel	ZR1
	V8	4.250	4.00	454	270	4800	8.5:1	Single four-barrel	LS5
	V8	4.250	4.00	454	365	4800	8.5:1		
1973	V8	4.000	3.48	350	190	4400	8.5:1	Single four-barrel	Std
	V8	4.000	3.48	350	250	5200	9.0:1	Single four-barrel	L82
	V8	4.250	4.00	454	275	4400	9.0:1	Single four-barrel	LS4

CORVETTE ENGINES

Year	Type	Bore	Stroke	Displacement	Horsepower	rpm	Compression ratio	Fuel System	Option Code (RPO)
1974	V8	4.00	3.48	350	195	4400	8.5:1	Single four-barrel	Std
	V8	4.000	3.48	350	250	4800	9.0:1	Single four-barrel	L82
	V8	4.250	4.000	454	270	4400	9.0:1	Single four-barrel	LS4
1975	V8	4.000	3.48	350	165	3800	8.5:1	Single four-barrel	Std
	V8	4.000	3.48	350	205	4800	9.0:1	Single four-barrel	L82
1976	V8	4.000	3.48	350	180	3800	8.5:1	Single four-barrel	Std
	V8	4.000	3.48	350	210	5200	9.0:1	Single four-barrel	L82
1977	V8	4.000	3.48	350	180	3800	8.5:1	Single four-barrel	Std
	V8	4.000	3.48	350	210	5200	9.0:1	Single four-barrel	L82
1978	V8	4.000	3.48	350	185		8.2:1	Single four-barrel	Std
	V8	4.000	3.48	350	220			Single four-barrel	L82
1979	V8	4.000	3.48	3.50	195		8.2:1	Single four-barrel	Std
	V8	4.000	3.48	350	225			Single four-barrel	L82
1980	V8			305	180			Single four-barrel	LG4
	V8	4.000	3.48	350	190		8.2:1	Single four-barrel	L48
	V8	4.000	3.48	350	230			Single four-barrel	L82
1981	V8	4.000	3.48	350	190		8.2:1	Single four-barrel	L81
1982	V8	4.000	3.48	350	200		9.0:1	Crossfire TBI	L83
1983	V8	4.000	3.48	350				Crossfire TBI	Std
1984	V8	4.000	3.48	350	193	4000		Crossfire TBI	Std
1985	V8	4.000	3.48	350	230	4000		Crossfire TBI	Std
1986	V8	4.000	3.48	350	230	4000	9.5:1	Crossfire TBI	Std
1987	V8	4.000	3.48	350	240	4000	9.0:1	M/A TPI	L98
	V8	4.000	3.48	350	345	3800	7.5:1	M/A TPI	B2K
1988	V8	4.000	3.48	350	245	4500	9.5:1	M/A TPI	L98
	V8	4.000	3.48	350	382	4250	7.5:1	M/A TPI	B2K
1989	V8	4.000	3.48	350	245	4500	9.0:1	S/D TPI	L98
	DOHC V8	3.900	3.66	350	380	4100	11.25:1	S/D TPI	LT5

A familiar enough sight over the past 35 years on American tracks, the Corvette has occasionally made its mark in international competition, campaigned by such men as John Greenwood — one of his turbo Vettes appears on pages 234/235. Greenwood was also to the fore in 1972 when the BFGoodrich sponsored team competed at Le Mans (pages 236—239), his LT-1 leading the GT class for some while. Over ten years before, Briggs Cunningham led a three-car team to Le Mans (pages 240—243). The Fitch/Grossman car eventually finished an excellent eighth overall at an average speed of 97.2mph, having covered 2350.139 miles in the 24 hours to record the Corvette's best ever result in the French classic.

TOP A Sting Ray out of shape is a lot of car for the enthusiastic amateur to catch.

ABOVE In the hands of Dr Dick Thompson the Stingray enjoyed great domestic success, winning the SCCA C Class championship in 1960.

ABOVE RIGHT Sheer muscle, Corvettes have the power to leave BMWs in their wake.

RIGHT Nothing but Corvettes. The venue is the banking at Daytona and the year 1969.

PREVIOUS SPREAD Sebring '69 with the competition too fierce for car 11. In the previous two years Corvettes had won their class in the Sebring 12 Hours.

LEFT Daytona '69 with car 18 driven by the infamous John Paul.

BELOW LEFT A modified Corvette heads to victory in the GT class at the 1972 Daytona 6 Hours.

ABOVE & FOLLOWING SPREAD The mid-1970s were not notable for great Corvette competition success, but John Greenwood kept faith, running distinctive heavily modified Vettes — the example shown here is being driven by Rick Manguso at the equally distinctive venue of Sebring, in 1977.

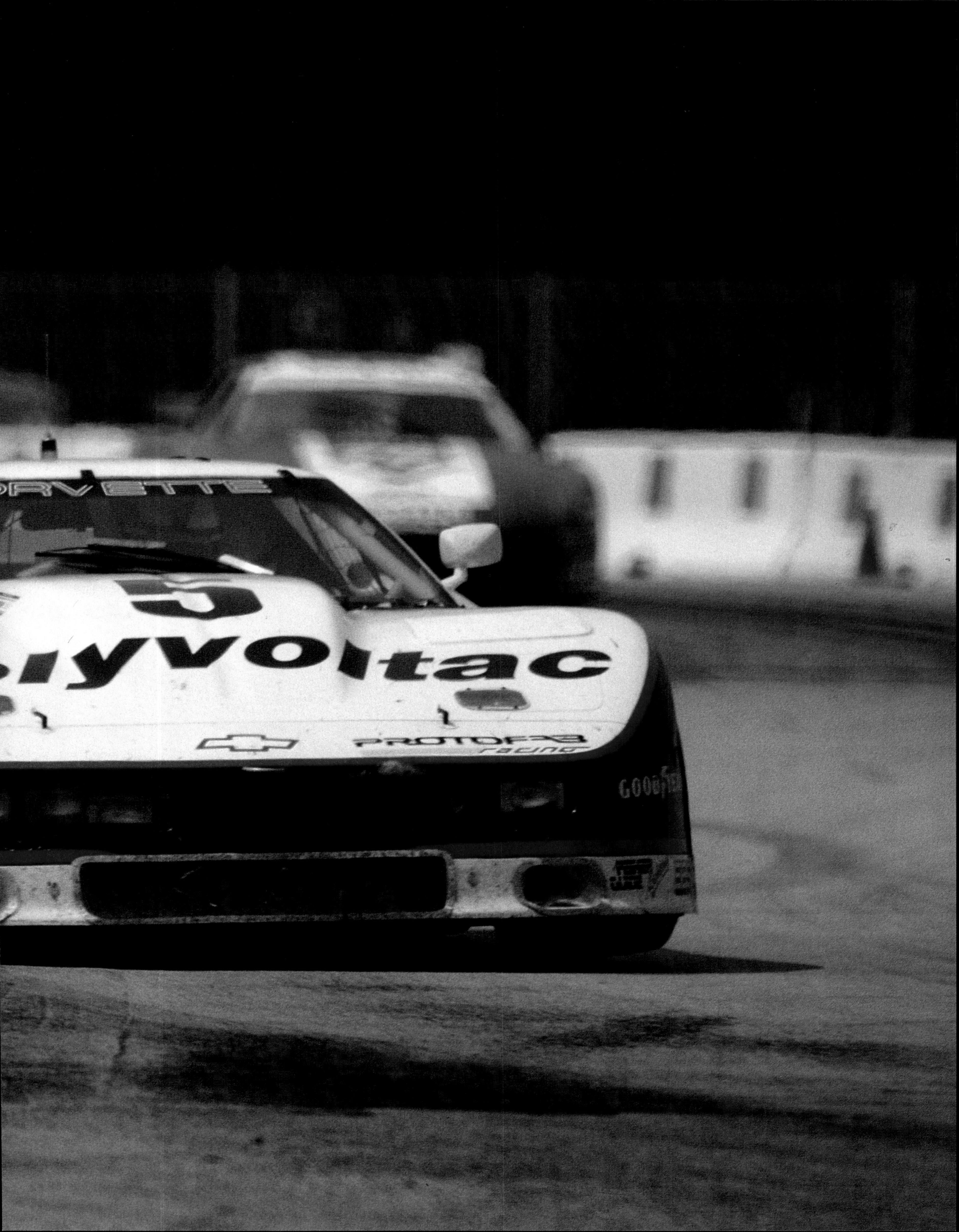
ORVETTE
5
lyvoltac
PROTOFAB
racing

PAGES 252/253 The Protofab team of 1988 ran this
Corvette in IMSA's GTO class with Canadian
Polyvoltac sponsorship. Under the skin is a
tubular steel race chassis designed by Bob Riley
rather than the stock Corvette frame.

PAGES 254/255 The GM Goodwrench-sponsored
'Corvette' is actually a Lola-based ground effects
racer with mid-mounted V6 turbo engine. It was
campaigned with great success by Doc Bundy and
Sarel van der Merwe in the IMSA GTP class.

ABOVE The Mobil 1-sponsored car was Chevrolet's
Trans-Am contender for 1988.

IN A CLASS
OF
ITS OWN

THE COMPETITION CORVETTE

BY the most accepted definition, a sports car is a dual-purpose automobile, capable of both pleasure use and competition driving. Yet, while a sports car is manifestly what Chevrolet set out to produce in the early 1950s, a true sports car was scarcely what they achieved. The six-cylinder Corvette was duly entered for competition in the rulebook of the Sports Car Club of America (SCCA), which in those days was the sole authority in USA sports car competition. But nobody raced it, or at least nobody raced it with distinction. Searching for somebody who remembers driving a Corvette Six at Lime Rock or the Glen is like old Diogenes with his lantern, searching for an honest man.

The six-cylinder Corvette was a paper tiger. At 235 cubic inches it should have been able to pace an Austin Healey, and follow a Jaguar XK120, albeit at a respectable distance. It didn't, whether because of the stolid Powerflite transmission, the cushy suspension, the underwhelming state of tune, or whatever. It was just not competitive.

The first-generation Corvette was not devoid of competition accomplishments but these were recorded only after the V8 arrived, and was fitted in almost all the model-year 1955 cars. Such a V8 Corvette set a class record in the Pikes Peak Hill Climb, although the Peak in those days was not an official blip on the formal racing calendar: USAC – the United States Auto Club, which would later become the authority of record – hadn't even been born in those days.

Chevrolet general manager Ed Cole wanted the Corvette to race. 'It wouldn't have been a genuine sports car if it did not,' Cole told this writer, 'but to compete, it had to have a competitive engine. As we were developing the [Chevrolet small-block] V8, the idea of using it in the Corvette particularly excited us.' The Vette had the right proportions, was relatively light with its fiberglass body; the idea made sense.

It made sense likewise to Zora Arkus-Duntov, who brought a 1955 V8 Corvette to Daytona late in that year to set a class record for the flying mile: 150.583mph. This, of course, required certain non-stock modifications, including a high axle ratio — but it proved the car's potential. Early in 1956, at the Daytona Speed Weeks, more fine Corvette performances were recorded in the standing mile and sports-car top-speed trials. The car's growing image as a competitor was bolstered now by another new factor, its revised 1956 styling, which gave it a more functional, serious appearance and was aerodynamically superior to the original.

It was the '56 that brought Corvette the services of Dr Dick Thompson, the Washington DC racing dentist whose Corvette efforts over the years soon became legendary. The '56 Corvette had been pessimistically slotted into SCCA's production class C, with the Porsches and Healeys; Thompson won the C-production championship going away. The 283-engined 1957 Corvette was moved up to B-production but Thompson — helped by the famous 'Duntov cam' (see 'Hitting its Stride') was unperturbed, and the Corvette was a national champion for the second straight year.

Few 265 Corvettes were run in SCCA races after the 283 came along, so it is not quite fair to suggest they made no mark in class C-production. Thompson's 1956 campaign saw the 265 Corvette out-point cars like the Jaguar XK120M, the Mercedes-Benz 300SL and the Ferrari Barchetta, which was good going. After 1956, B-production became a Corvette parade. The championship was won by Jim Jeffords in 1958 and 1959, Bob Johnson in 1960, Dick Thompson again in 1961, Don Yenko in 1962 and 1963, and Frank Dominianni in 1964. Through that year the small-block Vettes were invincible, despite some very formidable rivals including Porsche Carreras, Ferraris, and the occasional Jaguar XK-E.

It was Thompson's first championship, however, that was crucial in the story of Corvette performance. His 1956 win, and the publicity stemming therefrom, had allowed Duntov to justify the production four-speed gearbox and fuel-injected V8 which appeared in production for 1957. These two options did much to make the Corvette a true racing sports car.

Starting in 1957, the customer could order a Corvette prepared at the factory for road racing, simply by checking off RPO-684 on the order blank. This added such components as heavy-duty springs and shock absorbers, sintered metallic brake lining and quick-ratio steering to either a fuel-injected or twin four-barrel carburetor Corvette.

While cleaning up on the SCCA road courses throughout America, the Corvette also formed the basis of an impressive endurance racer. The first such effort, for the Sebring (Florida) Twelve Hours in 1956, was a four-car team headed by John Fitch, the famous Connecticut driver/tuning specialist. Fitch prepared a team of four Corvettes, using a production version of Duntov's Daytona engine with two four-barrel carburetors, the Duntov cam and ported manifolds. This V8 was rated at 255bhp, though one Sebring car, bored out to 307 cubic inches and fitted with a ZF four-speed gearbox, was entered as a prototype. All four cars were equipped with Halibrand magnesium wheels, driving lights and oversize fuel tanks. The end of the 1956 enduro found a production car driven by Fitch and Walt Hansgen ninth overall, while Ray Crawford/Max Goldman were fifteenth. 'Our performance was less than we had hoped, but more than we deserved,' Fitch said.

During the summer of 1956, Duntov built another Sebring car with an extended aerodynamic nose and a tiny tailfin on the decklid. This was Jerry Earl's famous SR-2, which was copied for a street version driven by GM president Harlow Curtice. The original, racing SR-2 was run extensively by Earl, Dick Thompson and Curtis Turner. Later, in 1958, Jim Jeffords took over, painted the car an ugly purple and dubbed it the Purple People Eater. It was this car that won the aforementioned B-production national championships for Jeffords in 1958 and 1959.

In July 1956, Duntov began work on what became the Sebring Super Sport or SS — a car that seemed great on paper but failed to perform in practice. Designed to beat the D-type Jaguars in Sebring's prototype class, the SS has a long, smooth, slippery body designed to cheat the wind, but it retained the familiar Corvette vertical-bar grille and body side indentations, which made its origin unmistakable.

Its form stemmed from a GM experiment, the XP-64, but, in fact, the SS was carefully designed for racing. As a prototype, it differed vastly from stock in dimensions and specifications. Its wheelbase was only 72 inches (the production car's was 102); its body was of lightweight magnesium alloy; it had a tubular space frame chassis, a ZF four-speed gearbox and a de Dion rear suspension. Packing the punch was a specially designed, Duntov-cammed 283 small block with 307bhp. Enormous exhausts tracked through slotted rocker panels and exited ahead of the rear wheels; a removable bubble top, and headlamp and side-lamp covers of plexiglass were installed to aid streamlining. The body shrouds tilted up fore and aft for easy access to all mechanical components, encouraging rapid pit stops.

John Fitch's team planned to give the SS to Argentina's great Juan Fangio at Sebring in '57, but by race time the alloy body hadn't been completed and Fangio opted out of driving the car. He did take the steel-bodied substitute out for a trial during practice, and set an unofficial lap record. This promising start was erased in the race itself, when the SS was forced to retire after only twenty-three laps — most of them run at reduced speed — owing to an almost silly failure: an over-torqued bushing. A production car did provide

some consolation: driven by Thompson and Gaston Andrey, it finished twelfth overall and won its class.

Also in 1957, a modified Corvette driven by J. R. Rose was an SCCA champion in the B/Sports-Racing category. And at Sebring the following year, Jim Rathmann and Dick Doane teamed to win the GT class and finish twelfth, repeating the 1957 performance.

Unfortunately for the Corvette, the Automobile Manufacturers Association had in early 1957 instituted their infamous 'ban' on factory competition efforts. This effectively prevented people like Duntov from applying the full weight of their experience to Corvette's racing effort. SCCA production racing was done by private competitors from 1958 onward, with furtive assistance by factory enthusiasts brave enough to take a chance.

Notable performances there were, however. At Pikes Peak in 1958, Ak Miller led the sports car division with an ascent in 15 minutes 23.7 seconds, an average speed of over 48mph — astonishing for the 14 000ft mountain with its narrow road snaking through 230 curves, a good portion of them 'straight up.' But the Corvette's true christening as a respected international competitor came in 1960, at the most appropriate circuit in the world: Le Mans.

Now it is not easy to chart Le Mans performances short of the overall winners. Every contemporary report of that race speaks volumes for Ferrari, which won an overwhelming victory: the red cars from Maranello finished first, second, fourth, fifth, sixth and seventh. Ferrari's only challenge came from the privately entered Aston Martins (one finished third) and the John Fitch/Bob Grossman Corvette entered by Briggs Cunningham Racing, which finished eighth.

Eighth is a long way from first — or is it? The winning Ferrari, driven by Paul Frère and Olivier

Gendebien, was clocked at 170mph down the Mulsanne Straight; the Fitch/Grossman (production) Corvette hit 151. The Cunningham Corvettes were also the heaviest cars entered, pushing 3000lb — and by a long way the most street-ready. Unlike the Ferraris, these were genuine dual-purpose sports cars. As such, a 19mph difference between them and the winners is less surprising.

Keeping in touch with a full-race Ferrari GT over 24 hard hours is not easy, even for a well run and capably led racing team. Briggs Cunningham's two other Corvettes, driven by Thompson and Kimberly, were running well at the 12-hour mark, holding sixteenth and thirty-fourth positions. But on the 207th lap, Thompson's car chose the pit straight to erupt in dense clouds of blue smoke, pulling off to retire near the Dunlop bridge; a broken piston was the cause of its demise. Later, the Kimberly car was pranged and forced to drop out. By the final two hours, Fitch/Grossman had the only Cunningham Corvette still running. However, another privately entered 283, driven by Lilley/Gambles, was close behind in tenth position, tailed by a duo of Porsches and the new Triumph TRS twin-cams.

'There was plenty of "cooling-off" excitement in the Cunningham pits,' wrote Bernard Cahier, because 'Fitch's Corvette came in boiling time after time. The car was so hot that it was refusing to start, so, to cool the engine more quickly, someone had the bright idea of bringing buckets of ice cubes. These were scattered all over the engine, under the critical and disgusted eyes of Zora Duntov.'

At one point poor Duntov had to watch this sole surviving team Corvette standing in the pits, while the next car, a 3-liter Aston Martin, picked up most of the nine laps that separated the two. Fitch's Vette nobly struggled back out, 'touring fluffily' as The Autocar said, while the Aston continued running like a clockwork mouse.

Just 15 minutes to go, with the Aston a lap and a half behind, the Corvette pitted again. 'More ice!,' yelled the driver. Ice was duly applied. The Vette rumbled back out, kept going — and made it! As the Ferraris slowed for a parade finish in an order long decided, the steaming Corvette came proudly home, boiling hot but still running — and still ahead of its English challenger. The two surviving Corvettes placed as follows:

Position	Average speed (mph)	Distance
1 Ferrari GT (Frère/Gendebien)	109.20	2620.773
8 Corvette (Fitch/Grossman)	97.20	2350.139
9 Aston Martin (Baillie/Fairman)	97.89	2349.339
10 Corvette (Lilley/Gambles)	96.16	2307.713

Corvette chronicles are replete with greater performances by much grander cars, but this determined showing in 1960 is one to remember. Against heavy odds the Corvette proved that it was no mere boulevard sports car, but a serious competitor in the toughest of all races.

Back in the Detroit trenches, not everyone was happy with the AMA racing ban, and predictably one of these was young Bill Mitchell. Now chief of design and a corporate power, Mitchell secured Harlow Curtice's agreement to let him race a car 'on my own time using my own money,' and quickly rescued the chassis of Duntov's SS practice mule, rebodying it into what he called the Sting

Ray Special. It was the first car to bear what would become a classic Corvette model name.

With Dick Thompson driving, the Sting Ray Special was campaigned throughout 1959 and 1960 as a C-modified car in SCCA competition. It was national champion in 1960, winning three times as many points as its closest competitor. Ironically, the Sting Ray never won a race outright, but took the championship through its consistent high placings. More ironic, the Sting Ray was really conceived more to advance Mitchell's styling ideas than to win races. Its beautiful, shark-like lines were soon being applied to clay models; both the 1961–2 tail-end facelift and the entire 1963 production cars were directly inspired by it. Yet it was a better racing car than the SS and many more pretentious machines that tried to keep up with it. One could say it was all things to all men: a championship racing car, a sexy showmobile, a pre-production prototype. In that sense, it remains one of the most important of all Corvettes.

The 1960s were frustrating years for the competition Corvette. Just as the AMA racing ban was beginning to wear thin, being increasingly violated by manufacturers; and just as Duntov began preparing his most fearsome competition car yet, the vaunted Grand Sport, GM decided on a strict interpretation of the AMA ruling, nipping the GS project in the bud. Had GM done otherwise, the Cobra might not have had the almost total monopoly of big-bore sports car racing it enjoyed that decade.

The Cobra was a squirrely beast, ninety per cent racing car, while the Corvette had by its nature to cater to a very large buying public which would never drive on, or even visit, a racing circuit. The Cobra was a problem — indeed a major headache. With the Ford 289, and later the huge 427, replacing the former AC and Bristol engines, the 2000lb roadster was tremendously fast, albeit hard to keep glued to the track. As a showroom seller the Cobra was nowhere — in its day dealers gave many of them away at under cost — but on the track, things were different. Duntov recalled: 'It was clear as day to me that the Cobra had to beat the Corvette. . .Shelby had the configuration, which was no damn good to sell to the people, except a very few. But it had to beat the Corvette on the tracks.'

If Chevy had built the necessary number of Grand Sports, as Duntov wanted, perhaps the Shelby challenge would have been answered. He was right — but he had the usual assortment of corporate bean counters to get by and in the end he didn't make it.

The Grand Sport was designed under Duntov by Walt Zeyte of Chevrolet Engineering, who started work in the summer of 1962, after the Cobra's initial impact. Unlike earlier Duntov specials, the GS was supposed to have qualified as a 'production' car under international rules, with a minimum run of one hundred copies but in the end, only five were built. The project was carried out in complete secrecy; even most top GM managers didn't know about it. Officially, of course, the company was still adhering to the competition ban. Actually, had the project been a success, GM would have banned the ban faster than they'd adopted it.

Built on a ladder frame, with 6-inch diameter rails, the GS was strong and very rigid. Suspension and transmission were stock Sting Ray items, but carefully balanced and hand-fabricated to reduce weight. Steering was stock, with the quick-steering ratio, giving only two turns lock to lock. Britain's Girling supplied the disc brakes — a first for Corvette — with aluminum calipers squeezing three pistons, two outboard, one inboard. The engine was an experimental 377-cubic-inch version of the Chevrolet small block (not so small at this displacement!), with an aluminum block and two spark plugs per cylinder. With fuel injection, it developed 550 gross horsepower.

The Grand Sport body was a miniaturized version of the stock Sting Ray coupe — itself just about to be announced as the 1963 model. Duntov thought well enough of this shape that he expected to achieve 180mph on the Mulsanne Straight — 10mph faster than the winning Ferrari just two years before.

Contrary to many contemporary accounts, the body was not alloy, though the 'cage' around the passengers was aluminum rather than steel as in the production cars. The body itself remained fiberglass, in Corvette tradition. Each body was specially hand-laid at Chevrolet, and made in one piece, so that it could be lifted easily on and off the chassis. The finished GS, thanks to extensive use of aluminum in the chassis was, of course, very much lighter than a production Corvette. The official figure was 1908lb, though actual curb weight ranged up to 2100lb with certain equipment installed. Nevertheless, this was still about 1000lb less than stock — a remarkable achievement.

Being ostensibly a production Corvette, the Grand Sport had a well equipped cockpit, which did not immediately suggest its single-purpose nature. A stock Corvette dashboard housed a full array of gauges, though an oil temperature gauge replaced the fuel gauge and the speedometer was calibrated up to 200mph. Deep, fiberglass bucket seats were fully upholstered and the floor was carpeted. The cockpit was completely finished and trimmed out, not spartan as in a typical racing car.

The Federation Internationale de l'Automobile — racing's international authority — indicated that Chevrolet would have to truly produce one hundred cars to receive homologation. In early 1962, the FIA had approved the Ferrari GTO in this same manner, only to see fewer than a hundred

GTOs actually built. Chevrolet, however, was fully ready to build the required number; after the first five cars were under way, authorization had already been given for another twenty, along with forty of the special V8 engines. The balance of seventy-five were scheduled for production, and would have been in existence by June 1963.

Unfortunately for the GS, General Motors top management thought otherwise. Early in 1963, GM chairman Frederic Donner sent an internal policy letter to its divisions, saying GM would stick with the ban. In February, the abrupt decision became public. Though Ford and Chrysler had repudiated the AMA agreement, GM would not join them. Donner's decision spelled the end of the Grand Sport program — the end, so to speak, of Chevy's Cobra.

The unfinished cars were sold to Grady Davis of Gulf Oil, Dick Doane, Jim Hall and John Mecom. These long-time Corvette racers then hired Zora Arkus-Duntov to prepare the cars — using, of course, stock engines. Duntov was personally still determined to produce a winner, GM or no GM. The effort was at least partly a 'factory' one, since Zora was able to get virtually anything he wanted out of Chevrolet, even though the cars were technically owned by private competitors. Eventually, Roger Penske and George Wintersteen acquired the two most successful Grand Sports, roadsters fashioned by cutting the tops off two coupes.

Because there were only five Grand Sports instead of the intended hundred, the cars had to run in the C-modified class in America. Amazingly enough, Thompson, driving Davis' car, ran fourth in the C-modified championships during 1963. In December, Mecom was in charge of a team of three factory prepared GSs sent to the Nassau Speed Weeks, entered in the same unlimited class as the Cobras. Using the special

377cu in aluminum engines, these Grand Sports were 10 seconds a lap faster than the fastest Cobras. At Sebring in 1964, the same trio appeared, but all suffered breakdowns. Penske won that year at Nassau with a coupe; Wintersteen, Peter Goetz and Ed Diehl combined to drive another coupe to fourteenth place at Sebring. In 1966, Wintersteen and Penske were still racing their GS roadsters, but by then, lacking any development for two or more years, the cars were hopelessly outclassed.

Of all the factory racers conceived by Zora Arkus-Duntov, the Grand Sport held the most promise. Built specifically to beat the Cobras on their own ground, they had the potential to succeed, if only GM had been willing to build the required hundred to render them as much a 'production' model as the Cobra. As it was, they did respectably enough, even though they never ran with their intended engines in place nor received full factory support.

In 1966, Duntov introduced his L88 engine option: a 560bhp, 427-cubic-inch big-block that was far and away the most powerful engine ever available in a competition chassis. This chassis employed the famous F41 suspension, with heavy-duty brakes and Positraction. Unfortunately, the production Corvette still wasn't competitive with the 427 Cobra in SCCA's A-Production category: the Cobra had almost as much horsepower and was lighter by half a ton. The only place for these big, strong yet heavy Corvettes seemed to be endurance racing.

Endure they did. Penske, Wintersteen, Ben Moore and Dick Guldstrand finished twelfth overall and first in the GT class at the 1966 Daytona Continental. The same team won the same class title and finished ninth overall at Sebring. At Sebring the next year, Dave Morgan and Don Yenko were first again in the GT class and tenth overall. More impressive still, Bob Bondurant and Guldstrand led the highly competitive GT class at Le Mans for hours, until their engine blew.

As the years and Fred Donner passed, GM's commitment to the anti-racing agreement faded again. Alas for Corvette, most of the underground support now began to go to Cam-Am racers like Jim Hall and Trans-Am competitors like Roger Penske, whose chosen mount was the Chevrolet Camaro. Chevy seemed to abandon the sports car classes to the unbeatable Cobras, moving to other playing fields where it had an even chance to win. Given the restrictions of the GM bureaucracy, it was impossible for Chevrolet to support an outside subcontractor the way Ford supported Shelby; it was equally impossible to turn a mass-production sports car like the Corvette into a racer capable of beating hand-built, single-purpose cars.

Towards the end of 1967, though, Washington's silly notions about regulating human nature began operating in the Corvette's favor. Suddenly, thanks to Ralph Nader and the safety lobby, Congress was in the car design business, specifying a wide variety of mandatory 'safety' equipment and (this more successfully) instituting controls on exhaust emissions. Meeting the new federal regulations proved impossible — or not worth the effort — to a number of firms including AC Cars. The Cobra was taken off the American market, and Carroll Shelby went on to produce a fleet generation of very special Mustangs.

Though pre-1968 Cobras still raced successfully in 1968 A-production, the lean days for Corvette were clearly over. These remaining Cobras were orphans, lacking a readymade supply of parts and dealers; the new 1968 Corvette body had better aerodynamics than ever, and with cold-air induction the L88 big-block roadster could produce 185mph; the roadster with its lift-off hardtop in place was more slippery than the new Stingray coupe.

At the Daytona Continental in February 1968, the first of the new, Dave Holls-designed Corvette generation were seen in competition. The quickest of these Stingrays finished tenth overall, driven by Jerry Grand and Dave Morgan. In April at Sebring, a trio of new Corvettes running in Group 3/Grand Touring ran strong from start to finish, Morgan and Hap Sharp winning this class. It was the first time in years that the Corvette had done better than something powered by Ford. This was relatively easy at Sebring that year: there were no significant Ford-powered cars entered!

But this happy circumstance would prove commonplace in the future, for the Cobra was dead. The competition Corvette, too, was an improved car. By 1969 an aluminum block version of the L88, called ZL1, was available as an option. This took an appreciable load off the front wheels, though the cast-iron engine gave more consistent horsepower through its superior thermal efficiency.

Corvette racing as the '70s dawned was shifting from factory entries or factory sponsorship back to 'amateur' race teams, though these amateurs were, in fact, far more professional than the old factory operations. One example was the Owens-Corning Fiberglass team, sponsored by the company that makes the raw material for Corvette bodies. Technically, this was an outside, unsupported racing effort. Factually, it had all the help it needed. Jerry Thompson was A-production champion in 1969; Allan Barker handled B-production; both drove Corvettes, the first time Chevy's sports car had been a national winner in six years. This marked the rebirth of Corvette production racing.

The old order changeth, and always will; Zora Duntov was nearing retirement now, and not possessed of as much determination as in his earlier days. Of course, Zora had enjoyed some marvelous innings; any desire he may have had

for fame in his field must have been well satisfied years before. Still, his influence was evident in the array of factory-built performance options. The competition Corvette was now the ZR2, a package essentially the old RPO-684, replete with 454 cid V8 (the LS-5 engine). For small-block aficionados, Chevy offered the ZR1 package, using the solid-lifter 350 small block (LT-1 engine), favored for Solo II racing or autocross.

Following Owens-Corning's example, actor James Garner sponsored a team of American International Racer Corvettes that placed well, but the real star of the Stingray era was John Greenwood, a combination driver, constructor, engineer and promoter, who brought glory to the marque and was something of a prodigy himself.

Greenwood attended his first SCCA driving school in 1968. Two years later, he won the A-production national championship in a Stingray. In 1971, he won it again, also snatching the GT class title at Sebring in a Corvette shared with comedian Dick Smothers. The following year, sponsored by BF Goodrich, he qualified faster than all other GT cars at Le Mans and was leading that class when he retired with engine trouble. In 1973, Greenwood and Ron Grable finished third overall at Sebring, in one of the Corvette's finest performances.

The broadly talented Greenwood even reorganized Sebring in 1975, after the American energy crisis had snuffed out long-distance racing the previous year. Alas by 1975, the enduros were dominated by Porsche, although Corvettes continued to place well. In TransAm and IMSA racing, too, the Corvettes proved too large and unwieldy to be really competitive. Greenwood's $100 000 'profile' racers were oversized Formula 5000 cars with space frames, fabricated suspensions and swoopy bodywork; but even a top speed over 220mph was not enough to compete with the twin-turbo Porsche 935s.

In SCCA production racing, though, the Corvette renaissance was complete almost from the year the Cobra was withdrawn. Corvettes won every A-production championship, and every B-production title with the exception of 1975. The most remarkable skein was put together by a Stingray owned by Allan Barker, which held the title in 1969–72; then it was sold to Bill Jobe, who won with it in 1973 and 1974.

The mid '70s were lean for Corvette, until a Stingray won the TransAm Category II championship in 1978, Greg Pickett doing the driving. Category I belonged to Jaguar that year, but in 1979, Gene Bothello's Corvette triumphed, with Frank Joyce third and Gary Carlen fourth in the Category I championship. Pickett finished second in the 1980 consolidated series; Eppie Wietzes was points leader in 1981, a season described as one of the most exciting in TransAm history.

The TransAm has, in more recent years, been the province of Ford's Capri and Sierra XR4Ti, Chevy's Camaro and Nissan's 300ZX. But Corvettes continue to compete with distinction. One such was Phil Currin's car, which finished third in TransAm points standings for 1982 — the last year of the old Stingray generation. Darin Brassfield and David Hobbs ran sixth and eighth in 1984, a season marked by impressive outright wins by Brassfield at Road America and Riverside.

The Corvette's long and proud role as an endurance racing car continues in the years of the 'new generation.' In SCCA's Showroom Stock endurance racing division, the newest Corvette has served well, winning every race through 1987, despite tremendous competition from Porsche's 944 Turbo. Another battleground of the present day is IMSA's GTO division, where Corvette won for Chevrolet the All-American GT Manufacturers Championship in 1978. Chevrolet has recently provided technical assistance for an IMSA mid-engined prototype, the swoopy, long-tail GTP. Lola-based, this racer bears a resemblance to today's production Corvette. A turbocharged V6, the GT class racer has held pole position for several races, driven by Sarel Van Der Merwe and Doc Bundy. Running under the Hendrick Motorsports Racing Team, the car is sponsored by GM Goodwrench (service) Division: it's a long time since the AMA's foolish ban on competition work.

Mario Andretti, in 1987, raced Chevy's Indy V8, another Lola-based car although perhaps not a true Corvette, for the CART (Championship Auto Racing Team) Indianapolis classic; the fuel system caused the car to pack in after leading for most of the race and starting in pole position.

There's a long, long, road awinding between that first, gingerly announced 1953 Corvette sports car, with its six-cylinder engine and Powerglide automatic, and the latest derivation of the GTP for IMSA. Facing a future replete with bright prospects for the competition Corvette, it is perhaps worthwhile to recall how it all began. How remarkable it was that this formidable racing sports car came of age, initially through a small handful of talented, dedicated individuals, and the resources which an enlightened management (most of the time) put at their disposal. 'Vive la marque!' as the Bugatti folk say: may the future be as full as the past for Chevy's sports car.

CORVETTE COMPARISONS

MUCH has been written about the new ZR1 Corvette with its Lotus-developed, 385bhp, thirty-two-valve, all-aluminum V8 which, it is claimed, will make it one of the fastest cars in the world, both in acceleration and in maximum speed. The fact is, though, that at least nine out of ten 1989 Corvettes will not be equipped with the LT5 engine package. They will be powered instead by the 5.7-liter (350cu in) small-block V8 which has been the chosen power unit for the Corvette since Chevrolet standardized on a low-compression engine in 1972.

The ZR1 version may be the so-called King of the Hill Corvette which is set to take aim squarely at the world's supercars, but it should not be forgotten that the 'ordinary' 1989 Corvette is also intended to be able to hold its head high in such illustrious company. The way Corvette engineers and designers ensure this is by doing exactly the same thing every other car manufacturer does when a new car is at the design stage — all obvious rivals are brought together, assessed, compared, dismantled, reassembled and put through their paces until everything that needs to be known about them is known.

Clearly the list of possible rivals for the present-generation Corvette was a pretty interesting one. When Chevrolet engineers sat down in 1984 to draw up a list of comparative machinery for the present Corvette, the cars they chose were predictable enough: Ferrari 308GTB (now 328) and Testarossa, Lamborghini Countach, Lotus Esprit Turbo, and three Porsches — the 944 Turbo, 928 and 911.

Other possible rivals, such as the Aston Martin Vantage, Audi Quattro and Mercedes SL range, were considered, briefly, but dismissed on the grounds that they were not strictly comparable with the Corvette's niche as a practical, two-seat sports car.

Doug Robinson, Project Manager for Corvette Development, explained some of the thinking behind such comparative testing. 'If we're doing a new model, we do this right at the beginning.

When we first envisaged doing the ZR1, for instance, we were looking at whatever was out there, and the best we thought would be coming over the next several years, to make sure that we had something that was going to be very competitive when it came out. We did that back in 1979, when we were doing the 1984 Corvette. We had everything — the best cars we could find out there — to see what they did and what they were like. It was a case of "fingerprinting" these other cars so we knew what we were up against.

'We carried out the exercise again in 1984, when the present Corvette body-style first came out. We fingerprinted all the cars again, partly in order to see how we measured up and partly to try to look into the future to see what we thought

these people were going to be doing. You're always trying to work out what you think the market wants and needs, so you watch your competitors and try to keep tabs on what they're doing as well as carrying out your own development and coming up with your own new ideas.'

The performance benchmark, from Chevrolet's point of view, was the Corvette. The standard L98 version, with its 240bhp, 5.7-liter V8 will produce a maximum speed of 150mph, and a 0–60mph time of about 6 secs, while returning fuel consumption around 18mpg.

So much for the theory. What are the strong and weak points of the Corvette's rivals and how do these cars compare with America's only true production sports car?

FERRARI 328 GTB

One thing all Ferraris have is charisma, and the 328 GTB (also available in spyder form, with removable roof panel) is no exception. In its latest guise, with 3185cc V8 engine, the performance of the Ferrari 328 is virtually on a par with the L98 Corvette, maximum speed being about 150mph and 0–60mph taking under 6 secs, with fuel consumption around 18mpg. Like the Corvette, the normally aspirated (non-turbocharged) engine gives excellent throttle response and scintillating performance.

The Ferrari's main drawbacks are typical of any mid-engined sports car — limited stowage space, fairly high mechanical noise levels and somewhat restricted rearward visibility. Despite this, the Ferrari 328 is an impressive performer which relishes being driven hard.

Chevrolet Corvette Production Engineering Manager John Heinricy summed up the Ferrari's 'fingerprinting' when he said, 'It's a nice-handling car and a beautiful-looking piece of machinery. It has a reasonable engine as far as performance is concerned, but for ultimate handling, not nearly as good as the Corvette. The Ferrari doesn't brake as well, nor does it skid-pan as well as the Corvette. It's also much slower on a race track so it's not nearly as aggressive a car. Probably its strong suit is its recognition factor in that it's a beautiful-looking Ferrari.'

FERRARI TESTAROSSA

This startling-looking machine is compared more fairly with the ZR1 Corvette than with the L98 version. Its 390bhp, 5-liter, four-valve-per-cylinder, flat-twelve engine propels the dramatically styled machine to a maximum speed of close on 180mph. Acceleration, too, is in keeping with the looks and should therefore be below 5 secs for the 0–60mph dash.

As with the 328, the mid-engined configuration means interior noise levels are high and luggage accommodation pitiful, while restricted rearward visibility and those very wide rear fenders can make it difficult to manoeuvre in tight spots. Such mundane considerations, however, are unlikely to occupy the thoughts of a prospective Testarossa owner for very long.

'It's another beautiful Ferrari,' comments Heinricy, 'and it's fast. It's more what we would be targeting the ZR1 Corvette at rather than the 1989 six-speed model in terms of straight-line acceleration and maximum speed.'

LAMBORGHINI COUNTACH

This is another conversation-stopping, mid-engined Italian supercar which is comparable to the Testarossa in performance and therefore also a rival to the Corvette ZR1. The 5-liter, four-valve-per-cylinder V12 which powers the Countach is an absolute jewel of an engine and provides a shatteringly impressive wave of power throughout the speed range to the accompaniment of a wonderfully evocative exhaust note. Performance tests show the Countach capable of a near-180mph maximum speed with 0–60 coming up in just under 5 secs.

The main drawback is, once again, practicality. Rearward visibility is virtually non-existent, particularly if an owner opts for that massive rear wing which has almost become a Countach trademark. The doors open upwards rather than outwards, which may impress toll booth attendants on the autostrada, but can be a little impractical in everyday use. 'The Lamborghini is an outrageous-looking car,' observes Heinricy, 'and a totally impractical one. Perhaps its strongest attribute is that beautiful-sounding V12. Its worst point is that you can't see out of the car. It's relatively fast, but not really that much quicker than an L98, six-speed Corvette. Granted, its top speed is a little higher, but the Lamborghini is a car we would target the ZR1 to beat.'

LOTUS ESPRIT TURBO

When the Corvette Division engineers did their comparative testing in 1984, they would have examined the latest Esprit Turbo, and that would have provided similar acceleration to the L98 Corvette, but a much lower maximum speed — just under 140mph.

Time, and technology, however, move on, and the 1988 Esprit will easily match the Corvette on performance and also achieve better fuel consumption into the bargain. The irony, of course, is that this close competitor for the Vette is another GM product, Lotus Cars now being a part of the General's vast empire.

The Esprit's strong suit is a long-time Lotus attribute — a tremendous ride and handling compromise which sees the suspension of the wedge-shaped, mid-engined machine capable of generating tremendous levels of roadholding while providing a wonderfully supple, controlled ride. Its weakest point is one of practicality. There isn't a great deal of luggage capacity, and interior space is limited.

'The Lotus has always been a good-looking car,' says Heinricy, 'but it's not a very practical car. It's not as bad as the Lamborghini, but it's close. It's very quick — about the same as the L98 six-speed — both in top speed and acceleration, the quarter-mile times being about the same for both. It's a very nimble, nice-handling road car and it's also okay in a race track environment.

'For a road car on the race track, it's not as good as the Corvette, not as fast, but if you set it on very uneven roads, that's probably where the Lotus is at its best. They're nice cars and I enjoy driving them, but you just can't see out of them very well. The Lotus isn't as comfortable over long distances as a Corvette, either.'

CORVETTE

THIS AMERICAN WENT EYE TO EYE WITH EUROPE... AND EUROPE BLINKED.

Let's get it together...buckle up. GM

Exotic Europeans have traditionally dominated the high-performance sports car class. But in recent United States Auto Club performance trials, the exotic American was the overall winner. The 1985 Corvette. So please join Ferrari, Porsche, Lotus and Lamborghini in a hearty welcome to a new world-class champion. The 1985 Chevrolet Corvette.

USAC Competitive Rank

	Corvette	Lamborghini Countach	Porsche 944	Ferrari 308 GTSi	Lotus Esprit Turbo	Porsche 928S
Total Points	21	18	14	11	11	9
Acceleration 0-60 (sec.)	4 (6.00)	6 (5.33)	1 (7.95)	3 (6.43)	5 (5.95)	2 (6.66)
Braking 60-0 (ft.)	6 (129.2)	3 (135.7)	4 (135.2)	2 (143.1)	1 (144.7)	5 (135.1)
Slalom (sec.)	6 (6.13)	3 (6.38)	5 (6.33)	4 (6.36)	2 (6.40)	1 (6.62)
Lateral Acceleration (g's)	5 (.91)	6 (.92)	4 (.86)	2 (.83)	3 (.85)	1 (.82)
Price as Tested	$26,703	$103,700	$26,121	$60,370	$50,384	$49,495

Scoring based on an Olympic system in which first place is awarded 6 points for each event. USAC certified tests, January 1985. All cars listed were latest models available for sale in the U.S. at time of testing and were equipped with various high-performance options. Corvette's Manufacturer's Suggested Retail Base Price is $24,891 including dealer prep. Tax, license, destination charges and optional equipment additional.

TODAY'S CHEVROLET

PAGE 273 Comparative performance figures say it all.

PAGES 274/275 The latest generation Corvette was designed to rival Europe's best, and three of its main rivals come from Porsche, in the shape of the 911, 928 and 944 Turbo. The 928 is nearest in concept to the Corvette in being a front-engined V8, but in Chevrolet's eyes is a softer proposition than their Corvette.

PAGES 276/277 Lotus have now reshelled and improved their Esprit Turbo, but the model shown was used as a benchmark for the '84 Corvette, Chevrolet aiming to match its mid-engined handling with their conventional layout. Ferrari's 328 GTB was another mid-engined exotic the Corvette had not just to match but surpass to make up for the Ferrari's enormous charisma. For years the ultimate exotic supercar was the Lamborghini Countach, outrageous to look at but with monumental performance. The Corvette can't match its four-cam V12, but at least you can see out of a Corvette.

BELOW A lack of practicality can be levelled at the Ferrari Testarossa but its flat-twelve engine gives it performance to match its looks. Nevertheless the men running the Corvette program are confident their quad-cam ZR1 is a match for it and the Lamborghini Countach — judged by recent magazine road tests, they seem to be right.

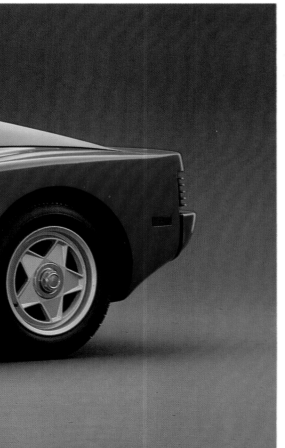

Having examined and driven the best that Europe can offer, the Corvette's designers and engineers have come up with this, the ZR1. It may not appear significantly different from the first of its generation, the '84, but a look at its powerplant hints what progress has been made in only five years. Where the '84 was powered by the 205bhp pushrod V8 coupled to an automatic transmission, the ZR1 has the 380bhp LT5 quad-cam V8, a six-speed transmission, and a top speed on the 180mph mark. Where to from here?

PORSCHE 944 TURBO

If one compares mechanical layouts, performance and overall concepts this Porsche is probably the closest of all to the present Corvette. The normal performance parameters are similar, as is the interior layout of the German sports coupe. Like the Corvette, and unlike many of the Italian exotics, the Porsche is also a reasonably practical machine which can certainly be used for day-to-day transport. Part of that practicality undoubtedly stems from its front-engined rear-wheel-drive layout.

As Heinricy explained, the practicality aspect is the main reason why the Corvette has never gone to a mid-engined configuration. 'In order to be a day-to-day car,' he says, 'I don't think mid-engined is the way to go. I know a lot of people don't use cars like this in that way, but they do like to take trips in them, and so on, and a mid-engined car is very impractical. Tight as the Corvette cockpit may be, you can really put quite a lot of luggage in the back of it. It's also a comfortable car to take on a trip since it has all the amenities. The heater and air conditioning work well and it's got a great stereo. The Corvette really is a thoroughly practical proposition.'

From a handling standpoint, the 944 Turbo has traditionally scored high marks. It has close to 50–50 weight distribution courtesy of its rear transaxle layout and is capable of generating some impressively high g-loads in hard cornering. The steering complements the handling, being nicely communicative and well weighted, while the gearchange is a little on the ponderous side due to the long linkage run to the rear-mounted transmission.

Despite the Porsche's excellence in most areas, though, Heinricy still feels the Corvette emerges the winner in a straight fight. 'When it comes to ultimate go,' he observes, 'whether it be the race track or the open road, the Porsche is slower than the Corvette. Even though it's able to generate the lateral acceleration, it doesn't possess as well set-up a suspension as the Corvette.

'The dynamics of the Porsche simply aren't as good when you start pushing it hard. It has a relatively unsophisticated strut-type front suspension and a fairly good rear suspension, whereas the Corvette is double wishbone at the front and has a lower centre of gravity. It's just set up to be a more aggressive car, yet it still has more amenities than the 944. The Porsche is a more spartan car.'

PORSCHE 928

This Porsche looks even closer to the Corvette on paper than the 944 Turbo since it is a bigger, heavier car and has a normally aspirated V8 rather than a turbocharged four-cylinder engine. Its maximum speed of about 160mph is slightly higher than the Corvette's, but otherwise performance is very similar.

It has often been observed that if Mercedes-Benz were to build a sports car, it would probably come out something like the Porsche 928 — solid, comfortable, an adequate performer, but somehow lacking in the excitement stakes. It may be the extra weight, or simply the way the suspension has been set up, but the 928's handling is not quite as crisply satisfying as the 944's. On the other hand, neither is it anywhere near as tricky on the limit as the classic rear-engined 911.

The Chevrolet engineers came to much the same conclusions about the Porsche 928. 'The 928 is perhaps best described as a luxury sports car', Heinricy comments. 'It's relatively quiet, has all the amenities, but really isn't a very good sports car from the standpoint of being an excellent-handling machine. It's quite fast in a straight line and has a good top speed, but it's just a bit too soft and flabby to be a real sports car.'

PORSCHE 911 CARRERA

This is the classic Porsche, the one that provides the link with the Stuttgart company's illustrious past. Powered by a superbly torquey, responsive, air-cooled flat six, the 911 delivers 150mph performance with acceleration that is the match of the L98 Corvette. Perhaps because of its long time in production, the 911 is also unquestionably the most uncompromising Porsche.

The rear-mounted engine provides both distinct advantages and disadvantages. The obvious plus points are traction and braking while mechanical noise transmission and on-the-limit handling provide possible points of criticism. One has to say 'possible' simply because many Porsche owners love the 911 for its engine note and the fact the handling can offer a driving challenge.

This Porsche provides roadholding to a very high level — more than most drivers are ever likely to exceed in normal driving — but when the limit is approached, the concentration of mass resulting from the engine's location will cause the back end of the 911 to step out of line very quickly. It requires a skilled driver with hair-trigger reactions to wind on sufficient steering lock quickly enough to counter the developing tail-skid and the pendulum-swing reaction. All of this is part of the 911 mystique, however, and there's certainly no denying the car just oozes character.

'The 911 shows its age quite clearly in some areas. It is pretty spartan inside and items like the heating and ventilation systems are really just not acceptable in this day and age,' says Heinricy. 'There's no arguing with the performance that's available, particularly from the turbocharged version, and the handling is sharp, up to a point. You've really got to know what you're doing to get it around a race track quickly and it's

therefore a much more difficult car to drive on the limit than a Corvette. The 911 has always been a terror for braking because of the rear-mounted engine, but the Corvette still produces better stopping distance.

'The real complaint I have against the 911 is the level of mechanical noise. Granted, it's quite an interesting engine note for the first few miles, but it really does become tiring in the course of a long trip. Once again, I think this is an area where the Corvette scores strongly.'

That, then, constituted the Chevrolet engineers' shortlist of comparative machinery when they were drawing up their blueprint for the Corvette of the 1980s. It could be argued that one or two other manufacturers' products might usefully have been looked at. The original Audi Quattro and the Jaguar XJ-S are two possibilities which present themselves. They were, in fact, considered but rejected, as Doug Robinson explains.

'We looked briefly at each of these cars', he says, 'but rejected them as not being real competitors for the Corvette. The Jaguar is a beautifully refined machine in the Grand Touring tradition. It isn't a sports car.'

'The Audi wasn't a car which particularly impressed me when I drove it. For some reason, you get a lot of vibration through the shifter with the lever bouncing all over the place. It might be because Audi's five-cylinder engines have a lot of inherent roughness and therefore have to be very softly mounted.'

''It' well known that Mercedes will shortly be introducing its new sports car', continues Robinson, 'and that BMW will be launching its new 8-series coupe. We're always watching the opposition, but we don't consider those cars to be direct competition. Even so, they might come out with a new traction-control device or a new kind of transmission that we're interested in, so we might look at them for something specific like that.

'Similarly, when we brought out the Corvette convertible in 1986, we had a Porsche 911 cabriolet, a Mercedes SL — those were the two main competitors . . . and a couple of other convertibles in for comparison purposes.'

An important point to remember about this comparison process is that these other cars aren't really rivals at all. The fact is, there are very few conquest sales involving Corvettes. The exercise is not about getting possible Porsche, Ferrari, Lamborghini and Lotus owners to switch to the Corvette, but simply about allowing Chevrolet engineers to keep up with the latest technology and, hopefully, with their own input, improve on it.

'We like to think that people who buy Corvettes buy them because they like Corvette,' says Robinson, 'not because they wanted a Porsche and the Corvette does a lot of what the Porsche does or because we've tried to put something in the Corvette which is like that in a Porsche. It's not that kind of crossover at all. People who are after a Corvette want a Corvette.'

That comment then leads to a final question: what is the essence of a Corvette in 1989?

Doug Robinson reclines in his chair and contemplates that one for a moment, then sits upright and looks you in the eye. 'We are trying to stretch the envelope in every direction with the Corvette,' he says. 'For a two-seat sports car, we want it to be the most practical, the best-looking, the best-handling, and the best-performing of its kind. That, however, doesn't mean making it the most expensive car.

'In order for it to be a Chevrolet, you still have to have a lot of value in the car. All Chevrolet buyers are very value-conscious people, and that's where the Corvette beats everybody. There's more value there for the dollar than anybody else can pack into a sports car. That's why we feel the Corvette fits Chevrolet's brand character really well. It gives you more than you'd expect from a $30 000 sports car.'

That philosophy may go some way to explaining why the Corvette is 35 years old and still unrivalled as America's only real sports car.

283

BIBLIOGRAPHY

The Best of Corvette News
Karl Ludvigsen (editor)
Automobile Quarterly Publications

Car & Driver on Corvette 1956-1967
Brooklands Books

Car & Driver on Corvette 1968-1977
Brooklands Books

Car & Driver on Corvette 1978-1982
Brooklands Books

Car & Driver on Corvette 1983-1988
Brooklands Books

Chevrolet Corvette Autohistory
Thomas Falconer
Osprey Publishing

The Classic Corvette
Richard Nicholls
Bison Books

The Complete Corvette Restoration
& Technical Guide, Volume 1 1953-1962
Noland Adams
Automobile Quarterly Publications

Corvette, America's Star-spangled Sports Car
Karl Ludvigsen
Automobile Quarterly Publications

Corvette, A Piece of the Action
William I. Mitchell & Allan Girdler
Automobile Quarterly Publications

Corvette Driver/Owner Guide 1953-1988 Models
Michael Antonick
Motorbooks International

Corvette Roadster: A History of Chevrolet's
Open Sports Car from 1953
Haynes Publishing

Corvette! Sports Car of America
Michael Antonick
Michael Bruce Associates

Corvette Stingray Super Profile
Bob Ackerson
Haynes Publishing Group

Corvette: Thirty Years of Great Advertising
Automobile Quarterly Publications

Corvette 1963 to Present
Richard Nicholls
Bison Books

The Corvettes 1953-1988: A Collector's Guide
Richard Langworth
Motor Racing Publications Ltd

Corvettes for the Road
Henry Rasmussen
Motorbooks International

The Genuine Corvette Black Book
Motor Books International

Illustrated Corvette Buyer's Guide
Michael Antonick
Motorbooks International

The Newest Corvette, From A Through z-52
Michael Lamm
Lamm-Morada Publishing

The Real Corvette
Ray Miller & Glenn Embree
Evergreen Press

Road & Track on Corvette 1953-1967
Brooklands Books

Road & Track on Corvette 1968-1982
Brooklands Books

Road & Track on Corvette 1982-1986
Brooklands Books

INDEX

285

ACKNOWLEDGEMENTS

The Publishers and CW Editorial Limited would like to thank the following for supplying pictures for this book:

Pete Biro; Jerry Burton; Chevrolet Public Relations; David Dewhurst; Louis Klemantaski; The National Motor Museum at Beaulieu, Hampshire; Bill Oursler; Phipps Photographic.

We are indebted to Stephen M. Chapman of Boston, Massachusetts, who supplied the majority of the cars photographed by Laurie Caddell specially for this book.

Grateful thanks also to Kevin Brazendale, Laurie Caddell, Alan Gooch, Sonya Sibbons and Ian Ward for their help and support.

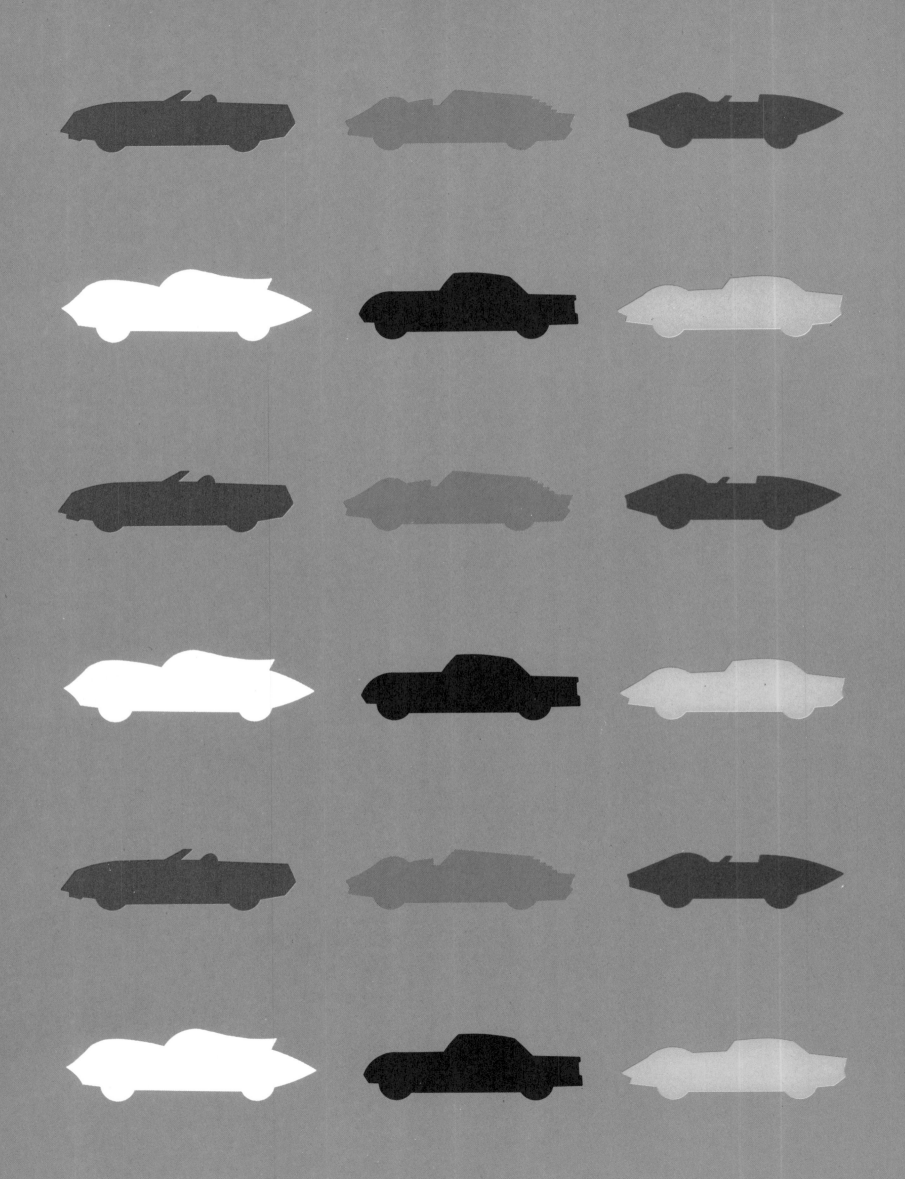